Sucker

Lana Citron was born in Dublin in 1969. A history graduate of Trinity College, Dublin, she has been living in London for the past four years. This is her first novel.

Sucker

LANA CITRON

Secker & Warburg
LONDON

Published by Secker & Warburg 1998

2 4 6 8 10 9 7 5 3 1

CIT
M02161

First published in Great Britain in 1998 by
Secker & Warburg
Random House, 20 Vauxhall Bridge Road,
London SW1V 2SA

Random House Australia (Pty) Limited
20 Alfred Street, Milsons Point, Sydney,
New South Wales 2061, Australia

Random House New Zealand Limited
18 Poland Road, Glenfield,
Auckland 10, New Zealand

Random House South Africa (Pty) Limited
Endulini, 5A Jubilee Road,
Parktown 2193, South Africa

Random House UK Limited Reg. No. 954009

A CIP catalogue record for this book
is available from the British Library

ISBN 0 436 20508 4

Papers used by Random House UK Limited are natural,
recyclable products made from wood grown in sustainable forests.
The manufacturing processes conform to the environmental
regulations of the country of origin.

Printed and bound in Great Britain by
Mackays of Chatham PLC

To The Underdog
with love

Contents

A certain situation

. . . something beginning with . . .
 Don't know?
 OK I'll give you a clue.
 It's late, it's raining, it's dismal dark and perfect.
 And . . . ?
 All right then, it was way past midnight and I'd just got in,
I ran myself a bath, fixed myself a drink and . . .
 Give up?
 You can't, I haven't begun.
 So . . .
 Strange . . .
 See I heard a muffled holler thought it was myself coming
from within, get out of this situation girl, you're in the
wrong place, wrong scenario and I raised a rose-tinted
curtain to take a peek, all the better to see you with . . .
 To see who?
 A he and a she
 And?
 Eye, eye?
 Did he catch hers or did she catch his?
 No matter, no matter, 'cause there was a dead end staring
her straight in the face and I see her hesitate, see her muse a
moment on the best form of strategy, her eyelids batting,

steel-tipped stilettos, well they're all the rage, tappity tappitying, her tight, short skirt riding high and it's two steps forward, two steps back.

She glances over her shoulder and pretends she's just noticed him. Like the good little damsel in distress she quickens her pace, he's loving it, has her rhythm down to a tee. She loiters a little, doesn't want her hero to lose her, doesn't want to make it too complex.

She hurry scurries nowhere, there is nowhere to go. She stops.

Give in? give up?

Good Lord and she's hoping you're keeping an eye on the ins and the outs, the comings, the goings . . .

Heeee's com-ing to get heeeeeeeeeeeeeeeeer . . .

Wait she hasn't reached one hundred, 98, 99 1 . . .

Of course they had it all planned out, they were just waiting for an opportune moment. And I'm thinking they're punch drunk and I'm thinking she's creaming up man, can almost feel his breath upon her neck.

Bang on and hand on shoulder . . .

That's the way to do it, that's the way to do it.

What the . . . Panic . . . shock and just for good measure she throws in a bit of a struggle . . . there they go round the Mulberry Bush, Mulberry Bush and she's scared witless, so she shan't scream . . . Hey and I'll give him his due, he's really going for it . . . not so rough you bastard . . . he's got her on the ground, is clawing away, her knick-knacks swimming about her ankles and I bet you she's cursing herself for not having put on a clean pair, what difference, what difference.

Oh God . . . Oh my God . . .

Time to go folks end of the show . . .

Oh . . .
Swish of a curtain to blur my vision.
And?
I know something that you don't know.
Hey, 'cause what the eye don't see the heart don't grieve.
And?
I'm a little monkey times three.
Swish of a curtain to ease my conscience.

No, no, that won't do at all, that really will not do.
Start again.

A day in the life

Oh to be deep in the heart of Winnie the Pooh Land, no really my back is cracking me up and I reek of the shit I'm immersed in. See I've been adrift a good while now, sinking in stinking Sewer Scum City. Like me forefathers before me, I only did what was expected and came to bleed off another state. That was all, I swear to you, scrub my mouth out with soap and water if it's not so.

So . . .

There's ringing in my ears and I rise and fall and rise, to slam off the morning warning and it's early, way too early, 'cause my face is out of shape and I go through the motions . . . can't be too alert or I'd never make it to the door but I do and what do you know a new day dawns.

I want the earth to open up and swallow me whole.

Compromise, compromise. Second best will have to do, as long as it takes me from A to B and I disappear down the tunnel and join the ranks standing to attention . . . standing just that little bit too close to the platform edge.

Thinking perchance of taking an extra step?

Hey, I could give you a push, help you on your way 'cause . . . Jeepers creepers but I wish I was rifle trained, it would be nice to travel in an empty carriage. Imagine having

4

civilised feelings first thing in the morning. A tad surreal I'm thinking.

Pushing, shoving, shoving, pushing, after that extra bit of space, cramped like the inside of my bowels. I don't want to do this, but I do, 'cause I have to, don't breathe on me, don't touch me and if I wasn't a coward I'd fucking well slice you in half. I'm thinking this must be a joke but no one is laughing. Congratulations and I'm awarded the honorary position of judging a most disgusting humanoid emission. A souvenir like, guess it's to do with my height, always bad first thing in the morning, worse when it's not of your own making.

Let the passengers off FIRST.

Dear oh dear but it would make you think.

To think . . . didn't I give up on that when I started earning me bread and butter. If only I'd heeded the advice of Marie Antoinette but sure wasn't I on a diet at the time, anyhow my bottom was of the wrong persuasion to even contemplate hard labour. I left the boys to their own devices and went in search of something more becoming to a fatal femme.

And it wasn't easy.

See I was impressionable then. A man in a suit stopped me in my tracks. Screeched me to a halt and compared me to the night sky above. Said it was only a matter of time before I joined the rest of them. Twinkle twinkle little star, says himself, leave it to me, says he, nothing for you to worry your pretty little head about. My besuited Seigneur and he took me under his wing. His big greasy wing, and beneath him I could feel his pockets bulging so I let him bring me out for a meal or two and . . .

No we'll not go raking up the past, well not yet.

It's all a bit tender, all a bit raw.

It's all a bit present.

Next thing you know

and a lot of water has passed under the bridge

Next thing you know

'Good morning I'm looking for Asshole Arsewipe.'

'Oh you must be the temp.'

She looks at me like I'm a piece of shit.

On the contrary, I like to think I breathe a little life into the dull reality of convicted 9–5ers.

'Ah Mr Allan this is our temp for the week.'

He shows me into a small room at the back of the office. Away from everything, away from everyone. The walls are lined with legal books, bar one with a small barred window which I sit with my back to.

'We want you to update our reference books. You have done this before?'

'Oh yes,' say I – got a fucking Master's in it.

I get myself a coffee and settle down to work. Updating, matching page numbers, tearing out the old, inserting the new.

Goes against the grain that does, tearing out the old, inserting the new. I like to keep a tight rein on my memories, some things just have that lasting effect. Besides, memory is the humanising faculty, see you got to retain a few to remind yourself you are one. My little life in onion layers, such times, such times, it brings a tear to my eye.

'We don't mind if you want to work through lunch.'

I'm not that desperate.

I leave the office and go down to the canteen. How do they do it, uniformity, conformity, Ormity, nothing is real, even the air is fake and they say I'm loop the loop.

I cash in on the perks of the job. A freebie lunch, a big plate of starch and carbohydrates in the guise of roast beef and Yorkshire pudding. It's Wednesday you see, today it's a roast and Friday it's fish. There is no element of chance, no surprises up their suited sleeves. Another good thing about temping, you don't have to talk to anyone.

I have a wander, a smoke and a read of the paper. Then it's back to work. You have to remain visible at all times. They have got to see what they are paying for, check that you are not taking them for a ride.

A ride?

Well more of a short trot really.

See he thought he was on to a winner. Backed the wrong horse though, sure I was a mere gelding at the time, all stirrupped up and no place to go. Christ I was green off the boat and it makes me sick just thinking about it. I thought I was being clever. I didn't even have to try, there was no effort made on my part, not a lick of warpaint on my face. So happening I failed to realise it myself, guys just have this habit of falling at my feet and I guess the only decent thing to do is walk all over them. Nah I am not guilty. I feel no shame. They just won't take no for an answer.

So what's new?

'How about an update on the updating,' chirps my cheery boss.

The table was spread with numerically ordered piles of papers. I groan a response.

'What would you do if I messed them all up?' He was trying to be funny.

I gave him a quizzical look, does he think I give a shit. Piss on them for all I care.

'So what do you really do?'

'I temp.'

'And what do you want to do?'

'I want to get married and look after my husband and have lots and lots of babies.'

He wasn't completely sure if I was taking the mick.

My besuited Seigneur and he said to me, 'The world's your oyster.'

I mean was he taking the mick?

Promises, promises, the world's your oyster but I found it distasteful and spat it out. OK I rolled it round on my tongue for a while, may even have chewed upon it haphazardly but it never hit the lining of my stomach. And now I'm left clearing up the mess, such a mucky mess.

Five o'clock and I leave bang on. Not a penny more, not a penny less. This is a week-long assignment so I say good-night. Don't want them to ring the agency about my attitude problem and I make my way towards Soho.

I've arranged to see an old school friend.

It's oh so boho, is Soho, cool, sophisticated with the best

caffè latte in town. We were to meet in the French House, some drunken media type will drool and then show us a good time. Really it is that easy. The drinks are on you.

Bea, pronounced Bee, and I have been doing this since the first spot of blood appeared on our knicker gussets. Our friendship scattered across continents, college and years allows us to be really honest with each other.

'Bea, you look great.' She was looking like shit, but was on a real downer. Her last lover had fucked her over badly. Though they had been split for over seven months she was still in recovery and it was up to me to lend a friendly ear.

'He said he loved me, needed me, could never be without me, subliminally hinted at matrimony, how could he do it, the things he said, promises he made, how, why, what, when, God she's so ugly, a slut, a total bitch, a, a . . . Christ I even swallowed.'

'Bea,' and I had to level with her, 'Donald is a complete wanker and you're well out of it. OK so you've spent the last couple of years being made a fool of, but for God's sake, give it up, let it rest, life goes on.'

'Thanks, thanks a lot,' and she switched on her sulk face.

I offered to buy a round and escaped to the bar. Five minutes later I was back with two gins and Brian.

'This is a gin and this is a Brian.'

Bea's eyes flickered and leaning forward she crossed her legs. Brian was to be tonight's wallet. He told us how witty, clever, successful and rich he was. Yeah right Brian, that's why you are a sad fuck who has to pay for people to talk to you. As if money would impress us.

I was hungry, skint and I let it be known.

'Have either of you two eaten?' I queried.

Brian smelt a shag in the offing perhaps even two, ye gads

9

his little heart was fairly thumping, two for the price of one and he offered to take us to Retzzo's.

'It's really good, I'm surprised you two haven't been.'

'Isn't that the name of the scummy guy in *Midnight Cowboy*?' says Bea.

'What?'

'Retzzo, *Midnight Cowboy*, Dustin Hoffman.'

'Ratso,' and I had to correct her. Bea always falls short of the mark.

'Oh yeah right.'

Retzzo turned out to be overpriced and booked out and what with the alcohol swilling in our stomachs we decided to settle for some instant gratification, McDonald's. Frankly we were not impressed. Bea started getting agitated, her mouth curling at the ends but Brian assured us the night was young and took us down to his exclusive club. Brian had spent a lot of money and numerous hours arse-licking his way to membership. We were not to be disappointed and we weren't. Bea and I had a jolly old time, Brian introduced us to a few of his acquaintances with a kissy, kissy, here, a whisper, whisper, there, stabs in the back and it's so good to feel one of the chosen few. He popped open a couple of bottles of champagne and gave us an inkling of the froth in store. We didn't like to disappoint, gulped it down, most satisfactory. Bea and I have exemplary manners.

'Bea if I don't go now, I'll end up in a debauched state in some stranger's room.'

'Don't go,' says Brian.

But Bea wanted him. She would regain her dignity tonight. On the rebound, Brian would certainly get what he bargained for.

And after a wait of only forty-five minutes I'm trundling

home on good old reliable London Transport. I'm really cream crackered.

Then . . .

Eye, eye?

Did he catch hers or did she catch his?

Something was amiss, street lamp lit, a bevvied-up crawler on the victim hunt, Tom cat stalking, squawking and from my perspective he's looking real good, well practised.

It was way past midnight and I'd just got.

I had run myself a bath, fixed myself a drink.

Swish of a curtain blurring my vision and I saw you, Mister.

Oh . . .

Then everything closes down and I hush up, my body gives in, awash in embryonic fluid . . . yeah nice calm time, don't have to think . . . I don't have to . . .

Hush-a-bye baby on a tree top . . .

The birds chirping the only time I hear them, past midnight.

Bea the strategist

The birds the beas, the sun and the rian
Bea   Brian
Be   Rian
B
Rian
Brian
It was meant to be.

Name: Brian Martin.
Sex: Male.
Age: Early thirties.
Origins: Distant Irish descent.
Religion: Roman Catholic lapsed.
Status: Middle class with correct aspirations.
Position: Media head (fingers crossed really interesting stuff).
Background: Only child to semi-detached one-car couple, mother, deceased housewife, father civil servant retired.
Address: Clapham, mortgage ?? . . . highly probable.
Salary: Uncertain but lives at least a 30k lifestyle (NB. mem. to exclusive club!!)
Looks: Average.

Dress:	Young, trendy.
Height:	5.8 almost.
Body:	Will do.

Love, love, holler it forth, shout it from the highest building, the Empire State or whatever. Human love and the spell was cast. Brian Martin had invaded her head, he was inside her, all over her, ohh . . . steady on girl. How did it happen? . . . she remembers, she remembers . . . she wasn't that drunk you know, OK she was . . . she was, she was slaughtered, but that didn't matter, what mattered was their connection, their spiritual awakening, that initial – er – eternal linking, like two golden rings . . .

One diamond . . .

One gold . . .

and a mischievous smile was over taking Bea's face.

What was he like? What was he like?

As listed, as listed.

Goddamnit he wasn't Donald and that's the important thing.

Brian wasn't Donald, Donald was:

(a) not Brian

and

(b) not the only one who could get a shag.

Bea had pulled, Bea had scored, she felt complete, she felt like a woman. Glancing over her list a hundred times or more, Bea reached the same conclusion, not bad, not bad at all.

Definite potential.

Brian was well on his way to entering Round Two. The seven lucky numbers had been requested and received. It was up to him now. Ever since their all-consuming, passionate,

13

lustful, meaningful encounter, Bea had stayed in on the off chance, just in case he would . . .

Dial, damn you dial . . .

but in her heart of hearts she knew he was biding time, sure it's not cool to go ringing the person you have just made love to within twenty-four hours.

Why isn't it?

Who made up that rule? . . . God it's ridiculous have you ever heard such nonsense, it's not as if it was just a quick in out and shake it all about, it was it was more than that, it was, it was . . .

Brian . . . Brian . . . Bea . . . Rian . . . his name tripping off the tip of her tongue, her mind drenched in daydreams and levitating above cloud nine, everything took on a new dimension. Bea laughed for no reason, sang with great gusto, her face alight with a smile. She gave to the homeless, made way for the elderly and cooed at kiddies in the supermarket. Even work became more bearable, she confided to her boss:

'I am floating Ian, I am floating.'

'Got a shag then?'

'More a copulating experience of the highest order.'

God he was so crude, so common, glaringly *nouveau*. Bea had been working with Ian for two years as his secretary supreme. Her mothering instincts were the key to her success and though extremely good at what she did, Ian relished in cutting her down to size, especially if she got too big for her boots and overshadowed his jack the lad couture image.

She looked over at Ian, he was grinding his hips up against the side of the chair, mimicking her in the most pathetic oirish acchent dere be . . . 'more a copulating experience of the highest order'. Cringing Bea was, her eyes rolling upward. Ian may have money, a great job and a dick but Bea did have her standards.

Since the age of fifteen Bea Mary Josephine O'Reilly had been doing a line with a steady stream of various potentials. She was in quest of a man. A man who would ensure a certain style of living at a level Bea knew she could become accustomed to. This was her burning ambition. Her only ambition. Her whole life had been geared towards this one specific aim, to enter the holy hallowed union of matrimony before it was too late, before she reached the precipice, the beginning of the end i.e. before her thirtieth, which gave her 3 years, 6 months, 12 days and a panic attack just thinking about it.

Every man to cross Bea's path had been subject to a rigorous check. Of course mistakes had been made, a few one-night stands had slipped through the net, but on the whole she hadn't fared too bad, having one engagement ring to her credit. The ring came from a certain Shay, a shy lad whose fondness for lingerie finally drove them apart.

Bea was not having any of that, thank you very much and Shay was ousted from the equation after a painful confessional with her priest.

'I stood there and all I could say was, Shay it just doesn't suit you . . .'

'And you say he wore a G-string with a lacy brassière on top, fishnet stockings and suspenders was it?'

'Yes Father.'

'And where would he be getting those from, eh?'

'From my drawer, Father.'

'No, no, what exact establishment would they be coming from?'

Three Hail Marys and a how's your father later Bea sat devastated with her mother who, more philosophical in regard to the episode, couldn't see the problem.

'It's just a phase Bea, a few good dinners in his stomach and he'll be sorted. You can't be so idealistic all your life, sure you only have to look in the mirror to see that no one's perfect. You're not getting any younger, you know.'

Christ Bea hated it when she said stuff like that, it was such a mother thing to do. Now don't get it wrong, Bea and her ma were the best of buddies only her mother was just about a zillion times more critical than anyone else, even if she was only doing it for Bea's own good. Ah the hardest thing to ease a diamond from off a finger and Bea had to concentrate real hard. Focusing on the thought of facing forty years of shared underwear and all that extra washing was not a realistic option and slowly the ring slid off.

Post Shay there followed a series of duds, minor setbacks and then she met Donald. Donald the dumper, who had left a certain sour taste in the back of Bea's throat. She'd followed him to London where he was doing a Master's in journalism, she'd practically kept him and then after two years of struggling he got a lucky break, started writing articles and receiving cheques for them, started mixing in trendy circles and then it was Bye-bye Bea.

Convinced of the right to annoy and insult him at any given moment, it was with great glee that she rang him following her escapade with Brian. No mourner Bea no more and the black band was cast aside.

'Donald how are you?' Pretending she hadn't a care in the world.

'What do you want, Bea?'

'You still recognise my voice, I'm shocked, Donny.' She wondered if her dash of cynicism was perceptible.

'What is it?'

'No need to be uncivil, I am just enquiring after your health.'

'I'm fine.'

'Really? I'm fine too, thanks for asking.'

'Great, no more tears at bedtime then.'

This underhand and quite unnecessary attack was made in reference to Bea's performance of howling down the phone after staying in for the tenth Friday night in a row, drenched in self-pity.

'Bedtime,' she retaliated. 'Chance would be a fine thing. I'm totally exhausted, shagged out. I've been soooo busy.' Bea aimed to convey the notion of being in a state of happiness due to hyper-sexual activity.

'Great, so what is it you want?'

'Now, now, is that a hint of jealousy I hear creeping into your voice?'

'Get to the point, I'm late for Crissy.'

That name, that crispy Crissy name.

'Oh the model with anorexia, a bit of a comedown

Donald, I thought you were more a tits and arse man.' Cow, feck him and Bea rocketed into gut-clench mode, saw red and retaining her cool flew out the window.

'Nah, that's why I dropped you: overdosed on the flab.'

'Bastard I hate your guts. *Guts*!' She screamed, slammed down the receiver and screamed some more.

Revenge, she wanted to do unto others as they did unto her. She ripped into a packet of double chocolate chip cookies and finding solace there demolished the lot.

Yummy, delicious and yous can all go to hell, even you Brian yeah, even you who hasn't bothered to call. Yeah Brian if you don't ring we're finished, OK.

Bea resented the fact that Donald still provoked such feelings in her.

Naturally she'd been incredibly distraught, heartbroken, had found out Donald was seeing someone else. That Crissy woman, the one who called herself a model, huh. She definitely wasn't as good looking as the pictures made out. Sure they used soft focus and retouched the stuff. You'd hardly recognise her in the skin. If you asked Bea, Crissy was actually quite plain, lacked character but if Donald wanted a bimbo then the fool could have her.

And it wasn't the first time he'd strayed, like a dog he was, a mongrel.

Love had a lot to answer for.

And as the hours trod by Bea's mind strayed further from the rational. Her sweet breads sea-sawing Margarey Dawing with, will he, won't he, willy, hee hee, he will. Her nails took the place of daisy petals and bearing the brunt of her anxiety were alternatively chewed to the skin. There had to be an answer, a logical explanation.

18

And then it struck her.

A destructive force was out to get her, the gods had turned agin' her. She was being punished for her sin. Her Donald sin. Things could have been different, should have been different if only

. . . if only the phone was free.

Ruth, Bea's flatmate was yacking to her sister.

Bea had been sharing personal space with Ruth since the split and was already beginning to hate her.

An animal-loving vegan, Ruth had advertised for a hygienic non-smoker with a g.s.o.h and steady job. She welcomed Bea into her humble abode, asking first if she would mind removing her shoes. Bea presented herself as a 'destitute woman', a Donald cast-off and Ruth, with her universal all-encompassing love took an instant liking to Bea the victim, envisaging long comfy evenings of mutual platonic giving. However, this was before Bea started going out. Before Ruth discovered Bea actually had a social life.

Get off the phone, Dog Face. In truth Ruth was a girl of great plainness, long lank ginger hair draping over features which clashed in a startlingly uncomplimentary way. Poor thing, she walked like a duck, had the arse of a horse and worse, was one of those people who think they have a personality.

Example 1

'and then I walked to the door but I had forgotten something so I had to go back inside and get it and then I had to come outside again . . .'

Example 2

'Timmy (Ruth's pussy) was so funny yesterday, he fell off the window ledge and landed on his back and he miaowed.' Ha, ha, she had found this hysterical.

Jesus but Ruth been on the phone for an hour and a half.

'Will you be much longer?' asked Bea politely.

'Excuse me for a moment Gillian, yes Bea?'

'I was expecting a call, I . . .'

'I have call waiting.'

As the night drew on Ruth remained on the receiving end.

She was doing it on purpose.

She was going through her address book page by page.

Had Bea pacing, sighing . . .

Had her in front of the bathroom mirror unearthing long-dormant blackheads.

Restless, her thoughts stampeding.

Sure hadn't Brian shared a cab home with her even though he lived miles away and hadn't they spent another hour in each other's company after the event took place meaning they had definitely connected although they were plastered . . . well she was but was he as plastered as her . . . or maybe it was just a one-night stand and she shouldn't have done it and he thought she was a slag or maybe he'd lost her number . . . her number lost and they'd never see each other again. A sharp intake of breath.

No, no, he'll ring.

Why wouldn't he? Why would he?

Of course it's so obvious, he must have a girlfriend, just her luck . . .

Jesus Christ Almighty . . . he could even be married . . .

Bea's little head in turmoil and her face blotchy red.

He isn't going to ring.

He isn't going to ring.

Get off the friggin' phone.

When . . .

Hark – the distant sound of a phone.

She heard Ruth pick it up and say, 'She's in the toilet' – Toilet, God yucky bodily fluids unbecoming to ladies – 'I'll get her to call you back.'

Bea started shaking.

'Ruth Noooooo . . .' and she threw herself down the stairs.

'Who was it?'

'Some guy.'

'Did he leave his name?'

'No.'

'Number?'

'Neither.'

'Didn't you ask who it was?'

'I'm not your secretary. Bea what's wrong with your face?'

'You knew I was waiting for a call, for Chrissakes . . .' and Bea was on a stormer, tears gathering on the shores of her eyelids.

'Bea, he said he'd call again.'

'When?'

Sensing her flatmate's inner angst Ruth took the situation in hand. She made Bea a lovely cup of herbal tea, put on some soothing whale music and asked if there was something she needed to share.

21

'Relax, relax, he will ring again, for sure he will . . .'

'Thanks Ruth, thanks a lot, you know beauty's only skin deep.'

'Pardon.'

'Nothing. Night.'

Snuggled up beside her pillow, imagined phone tones lulled her towards sleep . . . he called, Brian called, my Brian called . . .

But he didn't call the following evening or the night after that. It was not on, and out of spite Bea dropped a handful of Irish coins into the cap of the most miserable tramp she passed. Three pussy points had developed from her facial pickings and Ruth was deemed a turd face just because.

To cheer herself up she bought a chocolate cake from Waitrose and a bottle of red, settled in front of the TV and watched a film about a woman who surviving the trials of life – incest, gang rape, arranged marriage – eventually became a movie star. It was incredibly moving, incredibly engrossing. Bea could really relate to her.

And as the credits rolled the phone began to trill, once, twice, three times a lady and she picked it up on the fourth bell, almost four days, eighty-two hours nearly too late and . . . both of them trying that bit too hard.

'Hi, it's Brian, we met the other night.'

'Brian? Ah yeah, hi ya, how are ya?'

'I love your accent.'

'Charmer!'

'I called the other night.'

'Did you? I must have been out.'

'Up to any mischief?'

'That would be telling,' gushed Bea. 'Seen my friend a couple of times.'

'Yeah, she's cool.'

'Actually she's got a boyfriend,' blurted Bea with a hint of unconscious paranoia. 'Yeah he's married, a wife and kids sure he's practically ancient.'

. . . and on they chatted until a certain lull prompted Brian to pop the all important question. Brian said he had been asked to a gallery opening the following Thursday and would she be into going. Bea checked her diary,

'You're lucky, Thursday's free.'

So a date was fixed and the phone went dead. The conversation lasting a total of fifteen minutes which according to Bea's love-ometer was a good sign.

Plummeting up that cloud ladder Bea ran to her room, pulled out her wardrobe and stood in front of a full length mirror whispering 'I love you' to her reflection,

'I love you.'

Even daring,

'I think you're beautiful, no really beautiful.' She struck every sensual pose known whilst Jennifer Rush's ballad 'Cos I am Your Lady and You are my Man' blasted repeatedly in the background until Ruth asked her to lower the volume.

She imagined their meeting moment,

'Hi Brian, sorry I'm late, hi there, hiya, all right, what's new? How's it going? how's it hanging? Long time no see, absence makes the heart grow fonder. No be serious, be serious, this could be the one.'

23

Bea had a date . . . a date . . . a date . . .

Hallelujah,

Hallelujah

Halllllllllll...

..............eeeeeeeeeeeeeeeeeeee..............

..............................luuuuuuuuuuuuu.....

........................JAH

and she felt mighty happy.

24

The girl from the French House said yes

The following Thursday. A private viewing in a converted warehouse, Islington and Brian stood with a hand in each pocket waiting for his date to arrive. He hadn't envisaged anything to come of this most recent liaison, one-night stands rarely made it to a second date but an invitation to an exhibition organised by a woman who had cruelly refused erstwhile advances prompted Brian to call Bea, and loath to go empty handed, he had done just that.

Hands plunged deep in his pockets, Brian stood on the designated spot in fear of his initial judgement, debauched drunkenness can hardly be considered a precise rule of measure and he wondered what exactly he had let himself in for. His initial attraction had been due to Bea's overall largesse, which in Brian terminology meant a willingness to comply and ample mammaries, and Bea had scored highly on both counts.

He hoped Bea wouldn't make him wait too long, hated the fact it was almost a compulsory factor in dating etiquette. He'd wait half an hour tops, half an hour and that would be it. Times like these and he wished he still smoked.

Staring at his reflection in a shop window, he lick flicked back his hair, he was looking good, he was looking sharp.

Brian Martin was in his early thirties, just turned thirty-three, a fine age for a man of Brian's stature, five foot eight-ish with two-inch wedges which he hardly bothered to wear any more. Clean shaven he was moderately attractive, modelled himself on old cinematic heart-throbs the likes of Valentino, Gable and Errol Flynn, only with limited success. He had a small face, proportional with the rest of his body, small and lean so he made the most of himself, dressed stylishly in dark shades, flash designer labels, casual, minimal, very 90s, very modern. Image was important to Brian. As a youngster he had been an avid fan of the pop duo Soft Cell, used to idolise the singer Marc Almond. His mates thought he looked just like him. A hardly exploitable coincidence but he managed to work it to his advantage and the first girl he ever scored with was into Soft Cell too. He was seventeen when it happened. At a gig, couldn't remember the name of the band, or the girl's but she said, 'Oooh you look just like Marc Almond, I think he's gorgeous I do.'

A polite tap on his shoulder brought Brian to his senses and he swung round, flushed with apprehension and surprised to find two days' growth on an intense-looking bloke.

'You wouldn't happen to know where Basire Street is from here?'

'Basire Street . . . eh . . . first left, second right and . . .' and Brian stopped 'cause the bloke seemed familiar had set his brain back cataloguing at a ferocious rate, you know the face but can't put a name to it.

'Left, you say . . .'

. . . on the tip of his tongue . . . the tip of his . . .

'CC?'

Fucksakes it must be over ten years, more even.

'It is CC, isn't it?'

A blast from the past, a bloke Brian had once shared a squat with back in the days when he was a punk. It had been one of those summers that remain etched on your memory for ever.

'CC Arles, I can't believe it.'

At the age of eighteen Brian had cut up his clothing and arrived down in London to rebel against the system. He became a connoisseur in cider, dyed his black hair blacker and spiked it up with sugared water. He used to hang out down on the King's Road, time spent spitting and sticking up fingers at blue-rinse ladies, making a couple of quid off snap happy tourists and declaring 'Jus' cos they dressed like tha' don't mean nuffin'.'

He well remembered the time and remembered well a certain incident when CC had abandoned him and much to Brian's horror he found his physical stature a sore point when faced with opposition.

Battersea Bridge early Saturday morning, the pair of them lurching back to the squat, Brian stalling midway to puke up the liquid remains of his most recent Giro when two bikers whizzed by, two bikers whizzed back and CC, well up for it, turned out to be a fine sprinter whereas Brian's little legs didn't carry him so far, so fast.

It felt like he was at a Pistols gig but the only one pogo-ing.

'Brian . . . Brian Martin. We used to live together.'

CC rolled the name upon his tongue: 'Brian. . .Brian.'

'We used to share a squat in Battersea, a long time ago.'

'Sorry, can't seem to place you.'

'You shaved off one of my eyebrows one night.'

'Did I really? Dreadfully sorry . . . It grew back OK I see.'

Wince time and Brian remembered how CC used to take the piss out of him, remembered how he thought CC's arse was a golden chalice, CC the untouchable, Brian his summer sidekick. He could have gone on, could have recounted further misadventures performed on himself at the hands of CC, like the two tabs dropped in his breakfast cereal or when he was locked out of the squat . . . but CC stopped him.

'Eh nice to see you, Brian but I really must be off.'

CC had to dash, dash, balderdash and Brian though slighted gave him one of his business cards: ah well it had been fifteen years.

Brian looked down at his glow in the dark, precision time keeping, water resistant, terribly expensive watch and cursed. Bea was sixteen minutes late and the last thing he needed now was some cow to stand him up.

Seconds ticking and fifteen years since he had renounced punk philosophy in favour of adult maturity, or rather a job in a clothes store. The first rung of the ladder and it turned out Brian was a great salesman. He had the knack of gentle persuasion and was promptly promoted to managerial level. The clothes expensive had cute little labels which meant the clientele were of the 'in' variety, thus ensuring that for 10 per cent discount Brian was invited to some of the most happening parties. From this position he pushed upward and before his twenty-third had landed himself a rather good job in PR.

It being the 80s, selfishness was a key proponent in the feelgood factor and with share prices rising, houses prices soaring, Brian was on the up and up. Keeping his wits about him his vocabulary gradually extended to include such phrases as 'on account', 'taxi' and 'it's in the bag'. By the mid-80s what with sharp suits, polo necks and the birth of the mass-produced filofax, he was loving it, had rocketed to junior director of Image Inc., a top PR company run by a shoulderpadded Jay Goldsworthy.

He bettered his living arrangements and moved from Earls Court to Chiswick with Julia, his double-barrelled, Barboured, twenty-one-year-old girlfriend, the flat a birthday present from Daddy. Julia was rather taken by Brian, she called him her little entrepreneur. He introduced her to loads of dosh ethics for he was on the make, wheedling a mobile phone, voting Conservative and driving a swish sports car on weekends. Proud of bypassing college, Brian revelled in the fact he was a self-made man, cash happy and wallowing in it.

He reached a pinnacle then plummeted.

Some people remember Kennedy, others Lennon; for Brian the fateful day logged in his memory was the day of Thatcher's resignation. November 22nd 1990 and the company was going down the pan, accumulating massive losses, bereft of clients, Jay Goldsworthy's nostrils caked in powder and she couldn't get the words out fast enough.

'We're finished, Brian. Finished.'

End of an era and Julia found her attraction to Brian waning. Products having a built-in obsolescence, he no longer seemed so worldly and she started picking out all his bad points, like his existence. His limitations reached, the company declared bankruptcy and Brian was rendered a liability.

But as misfortune tends to strike in triplicate, it wasn't long before the next befell him.

It had been Julia's daddy's sixtieth birthday and flap flying about the flat, she was trying to find a pair of tights without a ladder when the call came through.

'Jules, it's my mother.'

'Oh I forgot to tell you she rang earlier today.' Jules regarded his parents as simpletons, terribly ordinary.

'Jules, it's my mother.'

'Yes Brian, and what does the woman want now?'

'Nothing. I've . . . I've got to go.'

His father's voice fragile, cracking up 'Son, it's your mother, she's . . . gone.'

Brian an only child was very close to his mother. The only time in his life they had fought was during his punk phase when she pleaded with him not to get his nostrils pierced. She needn't have mother-worried though. A compass through his left lobe was as far as Brian got on the piercing front before fainting at the jab-happy hands of CC. His ear turned septic and the hole closed up.

Brian's mother had hoped one day to see him married.

Brian had hoped one day to marry his mother.

Julia went off to Daddy's sixtieth birthday and Brian took the train home.

Not a happy time, seemed to last for ages, a best forgotten time and it had taken him a good while to get back on his feet.

Almost upright when Brian ran into Graham. A former associate of Julia's, Graham's rugby skills and more especially his ball manoeuvring techniques had been highly sought after by her ladyship though Brian had never copped on. Anyhow as luck would have it Graham was renovating a repossession in Clapham, needed a lodger so Brian moved in.

Boys will be boys and both out of long-term relationships, fun with a capital F was always at the forefront of their minds. PC in a laddish 90s way they were, theoretically at least, of the persuasion that a woman ought to be kept in her place, the place being the end of a knob, preferably either of their own. So they went on the rampage and once in a while they ended up with something, only on one occasion that something wouldn't go away and Brian was forced to seek medication.

Instinctively Brian rubbed his crotch while checking his watch, his date twenty-three minutes late, he was beginning to get pissed off.

He was beginning to get worried, his whole life flashing before his eyes and he sighed, disgruntled.

Brian hadn't had a proper date for a good long while, when suddenly he found himself being chatted up by two babes. Not one but two and he could have had both of them, he was sure of that, well that was his story and he was sticking to it.

Brian was getting nervous, Bea was almost twenty-nine minutes late. Thirty more seconds and he was going –

'Brian.'

'Bea?'

She was out of breath, a worried frown on her freckled face and a wide smile.

'Sorry I'm late,' she said. 'I'm never usually this late.'

Her hair long, hung loose, auburn to her shoulders, her face round, cheeks bulging with eyes brown, shining. She was a bit on the generous side, womanly, curvy, womanly with great big bazookas, in a tight sweater and pair of slacks.

Approvingly, Brian looked her up and down wondering how on earth he could ever have doubted his dick. Bea thrust her face into his and stole a kiss.

'No worries,' he answered. 'Only got here myself.'

He led her into the gallery, his arm gently placed across her shoulders, protective against the artistic onslaught, to free glasses of cheap wine and pictures they could make neither head nor tail of.

Durti gurll

It's all such a disappointment, such a bitter disappointment. Each of us trailing our dog dirt behind us, our careful agendas held in surgical hands, pooper scoopered, scuppered. Woke up in a sweat last night, bad dreams, black thoughts . . . dirty girl, oh you're such a dirty, dirty, girl.

Spied a certain situation, I tried not to look but it had a pornographic quality to it and you know you shouldn't but you do, oh you do. I was having a visitation. A disgusting, foul-smelling perversion was about to take me over.

It was that time of the month. Seigneurial rites to be paid in full.

Squirming I was, think of something else . . . quick, quick . . . in the deep blue mountains of virgin . . . yaaaaaaaaa . . . and lo and behold there he was standing before me, a brown paper bag in his hand and he tells me . . . his little bitty baba, he has come back to look after me, to take care of me 'cause I need looking after and he rubs his beard and says,

'Look sweetie, I brought you a present, a bag of sweeties for my sweetie.'

Ta-ta Mister, ta very much.

Yum, yum and I was salivating, all I ever hoped for, my dreams come true. Rescued. Rescued. In the nick of time, dream come true . . . or rather . . .

'Oh little baby,' he bills and coos in my squeaky tweaky eary poo.

Plead Misder doe talc dos big woords, Ied no very good ad dis, me jus a durti gurll.

What? what? he pushes his thumb between my lips, a soother sweetener for his baba . . . 'You like that don't you?'

'Sure I do, Mister.' Teeth clenched, soother sucker.

'Now, now, no biting.' Suck . . . sucking, sucker

Yum yum

And I bit his thumb off.

He didn't like that. Didn't like that one bit, one bite.

His mouth opened in agony and there was Bea, on his tongue, sitting pretty, wagging her finger at me and she says,

'Did your mother never tell you, you can't be biting off the hand that feeds you?'

Claptrap.

Yeah and I've heard it all before.

There was a time way back, long gone, before the cracks showed up when I was wholesome, when I was innocent when . . .

See I had a dream once. Martin Luthered on a star-spangled future but I was impressionable then. Anyhow a man in a suit stopped me in my tracks, absolved me from my own responsibility and all that malarkey. My options dwindled rapidly and that's when I started temping, sure you can't be holding down a full-time job when every other week you're being whisked away to Paradise.

Rewind to a certain situation and . . .

My Seigneur, a brown paper bag, sugar and spice and all things nice, all tinged pink and if I don't get it right this time, it could all go up in a pink puff of smoke. His left thumb and my lips eased open, easy now and he tells me not to be so obstinate, tut tut, tongue flicking, licking and I wrap my lips around it, right to the base of it and harder still. Devour it.

Thumb less no longer under his . . . the room went quiet and then suddenly I got real scared. And that's when the nightmare started, shudder to think about it.

Such thoughts, such thoughts milling around in mucky mental matter.

Bea would cross herself thrice, for shame, for shame, hopscotching fingers across her chest.

'Do you want to come to the Good Mixer tonight, Brian and I are celebrating our first month anniversary?'

Yippee and bully for you Bea, she sure does know how to celebrate in style.

'Oh you don't have to buy us a present or anything.'

Like the thought had crossed my mind.

'Well you're always complaining you've nothing to do.'

And the alternative is something?

So I finished work and found myself northward bound.

Camden Town, its ambiance hitting me full in the face as I stepped out from the station. Drew my breath and slipped some plastic into a wall slit, waiting for the money monster to regurgitate into my palm.

Headcase stood beside me and if it wasn't so funny it would be sad.

He demanded protection money.

From what?

From himself.

Said in no uncertain terms he could do untold nasties to me.

Oh really and now I'm interested.

He stood right up close to me.

Pulled up a stained sweatshirt.

Showed me how he'd been tracking time.

Life's incidents grooved up his arm.

He'd done it on purpose.

What?

I counted ten indentations, straight scars searing white flesh.

'No one,' I said, 'can have that bad an aim.'

'A cry for help,' he answered.

'Would it not have been easier to have used your mouth?'

He told me no one was listening.

Said, 'I screamed my head off, couldn't even hear myself.'

'They probably got scared, it's easier to blot things out, pretend they're not really happening.' Hey why the fuck was I defending myself in front of this jerk.

'Look,' I continued. 'What the hell was I supposed to do, I was in a certain situation and you just don't know what's what these days.'

He looked at me blankly, then asked for help.

Gimme, gimme, gimme.

The audacity, already I'd lost all respect.

'You're way gone, Mister.' There was nothing I could do. I opened my bag, stuffed twenty quid into my wallet, handed him an Elastoplast.

But Headcase wasn't satisfied, he wanted to tag along, had nothing better to do, nowhere better to go. On the edge, almost on the other side and he managed to cadge some money off a Samaritan warrior and he said,

'Cute girl, can I bring you for a drink?'

36

See it takes all sorts and the last thing I can be accused of is taste.

Bea wouldn't mind, her absorption point reached, oozing Brian and the thought of spending an evening as referee to the love doves didn't hold much sway, my absence would be noticeably unmissed.

'Where to, Headcase?' and it was staring us right in the face for there's no better place than the World's End.

Headcase had a vast thirst, so many troubles to be drunk asunder. He told me his history: too well loved by parents, far too well loved so he made a run for it, Dick Whittingtoned down to London to work in the zipping business, a fly by night to feed his meltdown action.

Well one thing led to another and I ended up going back to his place, a double-door shop front, his bed already made up.

The rise and fall of an Oxfam blanket, rough and tumble on a high street pavement, the well-heeled clattering by with a few token pennies thrown in for the performance. The dirty deed done and a good night was had, then on my way again and I guess I was feeling charitable, all giving, hey if the truth be known I was feeling like such a dirty girl.

The most unbelievably amazing guy since Donald

Ruth left a tetchy note on the kitchen table.

Bea, I don't want to be a killjoy but for the past few weeks, your boyfriend has stayed over at least nine times and at least nine times the toilet seat has been left up. I really value my personal space and don't wish to feel like an intruder in my own home. Please can we talk about this later?
Alone.
Ruth

A casual note, left casually in the fruit bowl, irksome, irksome, pain in the wholesome. Bea tore it into tiny pieces, then force-fed it to Ruth's cat.

On that night of a thousand stars Bea ascended to heaven and four weeks later she was still on a downward float.

Brian had been waiting outside the gallery. For her . . . and her heart pounded violently, her face aglow with sweat, sure wasn't she audibly panting.

Late as usual Bea couldn't bear the thought of being seen

alone in public, of people thinking she was being stood up, of attracting unwanted attention or worse, none. So she had it fine tuned to a reasonable fifteen minutes, allowing an extra five for first dates, but had ballsed up badly, having failed to foresee the tube taking a breather mid stations.

She thanked the Lord Brian had waited, and took it as a good omen.

After viewing the exhibition, their tongues loosened by bitter liquid, they left with the vague intention of finding somewhere to eat but hunger evaded them and brimming over with L.O.V.E. they city sauntered across the bridges of London, zigzagging the Thames, oblivious to time for it seemed to have stopped just for them and immune to the cold, for they radiated warmth like two ReadyBrek kids.

Ah how beautiful life was in the romance of the night.

How far they walked Bea could not tell, except it must have been a great distance as her feet wore blistered testimony, but little did that matter for together they had jumped dimensions, talked their way to dawn, surprised themselves with how much they had in common and of the feelings they shared. Their defences disintegrated, their hurting histories falling by the wayside.

It was. . .

It was almost as if they had always known each other.

They had watched the sun rise from Blackfriars Bridge, then tripped upon an open greasy spoon and laughed along with the lorry lads whilst enjoying a hearty, heart-stopping, slick offering.

'I can't believe we stayed up all night.'
'Me neither.'
'Bea, I had a really good time.'
'Me too.'
And as the commuter clan began to pop up like myxomatosis rabbits they tore themselves apart, their mouths awash in saliva, their tongues battling it out, kissing away the last morsels of breakfast and promised to call later.

Bea, smitten, skipped to work full of the joys of life and was, for once, punctual and on the phone to Ruth in nanoseconds flat.
'Unbelievable . . . No . . . Well more like . . . do you remember that band in the 80s . . . Christ what were they called . . . better go, Ruth I'll tell you everything later, Byee.'
Her boss appeared like a slap of reality frowning at the receiver in her hand.
'Morning Ian, tea?' trilled Bea emerging from a paradise dream world.
Ian grunted an affirmative, pig that he was with a trace of morning egg clinging to his moustache. He would on occasion tweezer his nose hairs, in the office, in front of Bea, flaring his nostrils so she could check to see if any had been left in.
'See the date didn't go well.'

'On the contrary Ian, it went exceptionally.'

'How come you're still able to walk.' Oink, oink and he laughed alone.

'Ian, unbelievable though it may seem to someone of your ilk, it is possible to communicate with the opposite sex without involving your genitals.'

Bea was always more articulate when in love.

Nothing mattered. Ian could rile her rotten and Bea wouldn't take it personally. Protected by a wall of love, she spent the rest of the day swaying ever so slightly from side to side, reliving the night in her head. Just thinking about herself and Brian 'together' was enough to bring on Bea's quivers and as she sat by her desk, her imagination roller-coasted until finally coming to a subtle conclusion.

'Mmmm, well that's it for tonight, see you tomorrow so,' she moaned.

The first date, the coming together of Bea and Brian had undeniably reached fairy tale proportions. If someone had told Bea she was going to have one of the best evenings in her entire life, she would never have believed them. 'How could it be possible?' she might have asked, but it was possible and it was true and she was really glad she had brought her camera. Spiritually naked they had meshed, though much to Brian's disappointment not physically, owing to Bea's mother's indelible words of wise caution (redundant in the light of their initial meeting but that didn't count 'cause it wasn't a proper date):

'Whatever you do, Bea –' and her mother had drummed it in – '*Don't.*'

Bea's face happiness drenched, for she knew she was on to a good thing. Her initial Brian chart, 90 per cent correct, had fallen short solely on the home front. His abode, turning out to be far below her expectations and reeking of 'unattached male' occupancy, had two major unattractive features, the first an accumulation of filth and the second, Graham. The latter had been introduced to Bea on their third date.

Graham was sat in a pair of pyjamas watching a porn video and eating a bowl of cornflakes.

'Hey Brian, this is good, man.'

'Not tonight, eh.'

'Oh right, the real thing.'

But bar Graham things had changed for the better and already Bea's first 'Brian' jotter was complete. A precise diary of events was recorded, everything of consequence and anything having a bearing on their future written from the heart, in neat handiwork. Ohh how she searched relentlessly for a mathematical equation into which to feed her facts. If only she could calculate the likelihood of their union, could highlight steps that might have to be taken, inducements that might have to be offered.

Bea forcibly had to stop herself from declaring undying amour, from throwing herself at his feet. He was everything, everything she ever wanted in a man. Smart, clever, handsome, witty, such potential . . .

Brian was definitely the most unbelievably amazing guy since Donald.

Four weeks down the line and the happy couple were in the Good Mixer, Camden celebrating their anniversary with a friend. They had hoped to make it a foursome but one of the party was conspicuously missing. Brian had thought it a novel idea to spread a bit of loving feeling so he'd arranged with a single, eligible and highly sought after mate to meet with a Bea female equivalent for a casual rendezvous.

Mid-90s and the art of giving is back in fashion and by Brian's well worth the money timepiece it was embarrassingly obvious she wasn't going to show.

Brian was doing his best to keep the conversation at a steady ebb while his friend Adam was feeling a prat and Bea, internally freaking at the thought of her anniversary being completely ruined by the distinct lack of consideration on the part of a certain cow, was biting her lip.

Inside the front part of Bea's mouth, just below her lip's lower rim, is a ridge of hard skin. Skin she bites to suppress moments of anger and inadequacy. Blood has trickled on a few occasions, most recently putting on a brave face when splitting with Donald. Donald was packing up, leaving her for good. Calmly vamoosing without a by your leave, without, seemingly, one regret. She had stood at the door, smiling sarcastically, biting hard, holding back the roar of anguish perched at the top of her throat. She was maintaining control and as Donald bid her adieu he turned and said,

'You're dribbling blood.'

Donald's last words.

'You're dribbling blood.'

Brian couldn't believe it, his head shaking from side to side, disbelief stretching out his eyes. 'That's one for the book, I ran into him only a few weeks ago.'

'Who?' asked Bea.

'Guy called Arles, an actor, Adam's representing him.'

'Is he famous?'

'Well he's gonna be.'

Bea was enthralled, a friend of Brian's working with somebody famous.

'*No* way!' she squealed. 'Jesus what's he like?'

'I used to live with him,' announced Brian.

'*No* way!' for a second time. Bea couldn't believe it, her Brian had actually lived with a famous person, wait till she told everyone at work.

'Way,' answered Brian drily. 'Back in my squatting days. We used to hang out together. I was just telling Adam I bumped into him.'

Adam and Brian had grown up two houses from each other. Their mothers shared coffee mornings and they were sent to the same Cub brigade and Sunday school.

Adam was one of those kind who had the knack of being brilliant at everything they did. He had studied law, graduated with a First and reached the top of his field in a ridiculously short amount of time. Gorgeous and clever, so rare to find in a man these days.

'So what has CC been charged with?' asked Bea.

'Unfortunately . . . rape.'

'Oh my God Adam I hope you get him sent down for twenty years.'

'No, I'm defending him.'

'Ugh, but that's terrible.' And her face crumpled in disgust, unsure whether she liked Adam any more.

'Bea,' says Brian.' Ever heard of innocent until proven guilty?'

'Brian,' answers Bea. 'Ever heard of smoke without fire?'

44

Like a good whiskey the conversation soon ran dry, so making his excuses Adam left Bea and Brian to further inebriate themselves.

'Clever guy that, top of his field,' remarked Brian rummaging under Bea's jumper, seeking a fondle of a breast.

'Huh . . . how comes he's single then?'

'He's divorced.' The sound of that unholy word sent a shiver upward through Bea's back.

Divorce, rape and pinching her pert nipple Brian whispered,

'My place or yours, babe?'

'Neither, I told you already Ruth wants a word.'

Thus the scheduled talk with Ruth was prepared for with copious amounts of Dutch courage passing through Bea's mouth and bladder. Christ but Bea hated being told off, made her feel like such an adolescent. So underneath the Arches, headed for Archway Bea stood snogging Brian up against the platform wall. Same line, opposite directions and she made Brian wait with her, 'just in case'.

Teeth touching and dribbling they lunged at one another. A longer lasting kiss, a whole fifteen minutes, their tongues getting tired so they cursed the state of public transport. Then tube-boarded Bea pressed her lips up against the closing doors and slurred,

'Mish you.'

She blew Brian a kiss.

'Mish you, too,' and he blew her one back.

Brian Martin, get a grip. Fuck sakes if anyone had seen him.

He looked around the station platform, safe he was quite safe, he hadn't been seen, ha, ha blowing a namby-pamby kiss and he reckoned he'd never done that before.

45

From the pathway Bea could see the light on in the lounge, Ruth was waiting up for her pretending to be engrossed in *Newsnight*.

'Is that you, Bea?' she called out.

No it's the big black bogeyman come to get you and rip you up.

For all the contempt Bea showed Ruth there was a common bond, a washing machine, TV video, microwave and central heating inclusive in the rent. Ruth was sitting in her armchair, in her house dungarees, stroking her pussy and scoffing at the political situation. Feigning surprise as if she had somehow forgotten about the 'scheduled talk', like it had slipped her memory while Bea, ready for the scolding, sat sulking on the sofa.

Bea crossed her arms prepared for the verbal onslaught, and her legs to suppress a swelling pee pain.

'Look Bea, let's get a few things straight. I share my flat with you, not Brian. It's OK if he stays occasionally but nine nights in a row is not on.'

'It washn't in a row.'

'All right then, you stayed at his one night.'

'OK Ruth I get the messhage.'

'Look I don't want to fall out with you, Bea.'

Ruth was such a self-righteous opinionated twerp. May her cat choke on paper puke, her soya be spiced with mad cow juice and her organic yoghurts explode in her face . . .

'Look to show you I don't harbour any hard feelings, let's have a dinner party.'

'Pardon?'

'Well what do you think? I'll do the cooking and you can invite whoever you want.'

Bea was beginning to get it. The poor girl had no friends

and was praying that on the off chance Brian might have a single accomplice. 'I'll think about it, Ruth.'

Bea did think about it, she decided it would be quite a laugh, she told Brian to be over at hers on Saturday for eight and to bring Graham with him.

As of yet there had been no mention of the love word, but all in good time. It would happen within the next few months. Brian would get so pissed he'd vomit, and out of his mind and in his weakness, he would belch out the words, I love you Bea, and Bea, mopping up his mess would feel perfect. Sex was already improving, they made love as many times as possible, with the light on, fully naked, in different locations and positions, though the utterance of those three little words would nevertheless add some zest and guarantee wild abandonment for at least another while. But for the moment it was rosy, it was sweet smelling easy.

The zebra crossing

An evening of loose linking stutters and Adam stumbled out of the pub tripping on the step he always forgot. Shit but it's so very cold this time of year and he pulled his wool coat close up against him. It was good to see Brian happy and Adam laughed at Brian's failed attempt to fix him up, and again he laughed at his own miserable third-party status.

He rounded the corner on to Parkway, quickening his pace, his car parked by Primrose Hill, the air would do him good, he was slightly over the limit.

His day playing in his head, his mind full of it.

'My client has every right to privacy. No comment, no comment, just keep your mouth shut.'

'Sure Adam.'

'What does CC stand for?'

'Nothing, my name is Richard, it stands for nothing.'

CC had sat smoking, his legs stretched out, ankles crossed. He looked like an actor, had that certain presence about himself.

'The whole thing is totally out of proportion.'

'How do you mean?' asked Adam, listening, taking notes, his left elbow leaning on the table, his left fist loosely scrunched as he rubbed an index finger back and across his mouth.

48

'So obvious, so sad, so little sparrow girl bite off more than she could chew.'

'I don't understand.'

'Listen, it was bound to happen.'

'What was bound to happen?

'Nothing that shouldn't have, nothing unexpected.'

Adam had watched CC perform in a couple of West End plays. Recently CC had hit the big time playing the lead in a successful film, seemed predestined for Hollywood, and now this.

People astounded Adam. The webs of mistruths they entangled themselves in, burrowing themselves into blacker than black tunnels. Lost in a maze and amazed then, when their heads pop out and the boys in blue are waiting, swearing blind it wasn't me sir, pointing fingers in the opposite direction.

Do your best guv, a nod and a wink in the wig man's ear. Ear wig and no remorse, as if it didn't happen, convincing themselves of their greater truth, their faultlessness, truly believing in their own innocence.

It wasn't like that.

How many lies had he heard in all honesty. Honestly? And how stupid can one be? Very. Blind to reality, 'cause it's a personal thing, reality, it's your own little world.

Hayley had made Adam feel stupid, she had fooled him into thinking she loved him, or rather duped him into loving her.

Either way she had made a mockery of him. No that's neither fair nor true, perhaps Hayley had just been the more honest of the two and Adam misled had continued in his love of her.

He had reached the end of Parkway and turned the corner. Turned over a new leaf, an untarnished page just waiting to be stained.

His boot kicked a can, sent it hurtling down the path and he watched its voyage towards a clogged-up gutter. Tabloid tittle-tattle, he had warned CC the press would be at his heels sniffing, nothing left uncovered and he pressed on.

A thin lining of frost on the ground, a line of drawn curtains at eye level . . . hiding the light . . . the crunch of the frozen crust, cracks in the pavement, in his story, forced, forceful, how far can one go, nearly there . . . fifty yards or so . . . all the way.

He sighed whiskey breath popped a mint in his mouth to make his thoughts more fragrant. His car stood alone, the last to be collected.

The last one, two dry tarmac patches, at the front and back of his car. His hand in his pocket, finger looping a key ring, loop the loop, withdrawn, then pressed the button and the car door unlocked.

Adam's back hit the seat. He placed his briefcase on the passenger side, had briefed his client on his situation, put the key in the ignition and turned the engine on. An automatic and automatically he reached over to the glove department selected a cd and inserted it. He had warned his client it was just routine, unceasing questions, boring no doubt but so many more and all to be answered and all boring a hole in Adam's head.

His right foot pushed down on the accelerator and he released the handbrake. He was in first gear pushing out, his lights on, look to the left, no cars coming, indicator flashing and out he moved.

Hayley had moved out with Ben. They hadn't spoken for over a year, two years since the papers had been filed, received and refiled. Adam had shut her out, cut her away like a ripe verruca, all the roots pulled from his body.

Freeze frozen.

Shit and it's always so cold this time of year.

It's hard to grieve the living. Hayley had remarried, in the end she married Ben's father and Adam had buried himself in his work, bookwormed his way through legal tomes. It was all paying off, it would all work out for the best.

All clear, no oncoming traffic. Top of his field and he half smiled half laughed, sighed. It's no good doing things by half, all or nothing. Nothing and he slipped into second gear, went up to thirty miles per hour, thirty-four years of age, slipped into third, thirty-five. His mind was doing ninety, he really should relax, unwind. His head cluttered and he looked . . .

. . . a head

. . . a shape stepped on to the zebra crossing, too slow, on purpose, small slowed down steps to slow down car. He tensed the back of his neck, rolled his shoulders and watched her, face down, huddled up, scarf and hat, big fur coat, boots to knees . . . he revved his engine to give her a start, move along lady. He honked the horn to dissipate the word Hayley which was scratched on his brain . . . honked his horn to move along lady move along.

A moment of time stretched to capacity, she took him by surprise.

She returned his start with one of her own. He had honked his horn and wrenched her from a dream. A dream a million miles from crossing a zebra crossing on a winter evening when it's coldest of all and you're tired of black nights and days of artificial light. He brought her back to where she didn't want to be and as she swooped her neck around in an owl-like movement he caught a blurred imprint of a face in motion, heart-shaped; pale eyes set deep red lips like the red sea opening and he looked into her mouth and passed down her throat over her slippery tongue that lashed him.

'Hey Mister what the fuck do you think you're doing.'

Her anger shattered his, smashed his windscreen with spittle, her words rattling down the road, a pebble along the pavement. Standing still a second, the last one, in front of his car and she looked him in the eye, her hand resting on his bonnet, commander of the moment, lit up by his headlights, buried deep in winter's garb then turned and walked forward.

Adam shifted gear, accelerated, sighed and again sighed

and sighed again. Accelerated harder still; his foot hitting the floor, he roared down the road and dissolved into traffic.

Hayley wrote to tell him she was getting remarried. An eight-line letter on textured cream paper. Hayley kept it succinct, didn't want to dredge up what had already been dredged a million times before. She said it was for the best, though Ben still missed Adam terribly.

And all too soon he was safe home, his flashing answerphone and a red bill waiting. He pressed play:

'Adam, Mum here, just to remind you, we expect to see you on Sunday for around two, Mrs Summers is coming with her daughter, I think. Looking forward to seeing you, hope all's well.'

Rewind, unwind and he loosened his tie, unbuttoned his shirt, poured himself a whiskey. Eyes closed he took a sip, sat on the sofa, kicked off his shoes and switched on the TV. A late-night discussion, a fat American with a very bad facelift was talking to a reformed alcoholic wife batterer:

'So let's get this straight for the record, after you hospitalised your wife for the tenth time in two years, and members of the audience, she was in a coma and on a life support system, you realised you needed help?'

The sound of an audience back clapping and Adam switched it off. He'd had such a rough day, was in need of a treat to rid himself of tensions, a bit of pleasurable company, to ease the morning forward. And he was glad he'd taken precautions, glad he had made arrangements in advance, a little something to ensure nocturnal entertainment.

Company expected and he raised the tumbler to his lips, to lick sip and took out his wallet and counted his cash.

It's the little things that count, I'm counting on you said CC, as long as you're honest we can construct a case, distil the truth, an ambered glass raised, the colour of warmth, playing with fire . . .

Adam lit a cigarette, pulled on it hard, blew out the smoke, to shroud the facts, to blur his vision, a zebra crossing girl blanketed against the cold, screaming her head off.

The buzzer buzzing, his lady awaiting, bang on time.

He buzzed her up. Heard her mounting footsteps on the stairway. He wondered what she would look like, his lucky dip.

Roll up, roll up take a chance and Adam had dipped his arm down into a crêpe-covered wastepaper basket, hoping to yield a return from a Sunday school fête. Brian and himself woggled toggled out, helping sour faced Jones on the secondhand book stall. He had wanted to help on the cake stall, he definitely remembered that 'cause the cake stall always sold out fastest. He had asked Brian to keep sketch, said he'd not be long gone. Seduced by the lucky dip in the corner of the hall. Trusting to fate as he slipped his hand inside, what will you get for your shiny tenpence piece, the remnants of a Christmas cracker or a star prize. He'd fished out a magnifying glass, eye, eye and what are you up to young one? eh eh? Brian snitched, sourface Jones snatched

the glass, marched him back to the stall all in good time son,
OK? eh?

Adam blinked, opened the door and an attractive woman
leant over to kiss him on the cheek, as if they were
acquaintances. She walked confidently into the room and sat
down.

He offered her a drink: 'Is whiskey OK?'

'Sure whiskey would be nice.'

And he wondered if she'd ever come across CC Arles.

The besuited Seigneur

Marcus was tired, his flight had been delayed, Frankfurt duty-free for over two hours, two hours too long. He'd come direct from the airport, had taken his time, it had taken some time to get where he was. Marcus didn't have to rush any more. He could afford to take things in his stride. And such a handsomely attired stride it was. Immaculate tailored suit, handmade shoes, greying hair, dark eyes, sculpted beard. Sleek, assured and at his own pace.

Distinguished.

A very distinguished black Mercedes with leather interior, wooden dashboard and peak-capped driver wound its way homeward. Overtaking in the fast lane, so much horsepower, so much comfort. Marcus's ears popped, he pinched his nose, closed his mouth and forced an outward breath to strike an equilibrium. He liked things just so.

Winter wet and city bound they were forced to stall in traffic, snailed back to his pad, westward, Westway, Singapore to Holland Park, came to a halt down a dead end, but very expensive. Marcus stretched his legs, yawned, stretched his Marcus mouth.

A cashmere coat hung upon his arm, house keys held in black leather gloves, protecting manicured hands and he thanked the contract driver. Dark and cold no house lights on. She must be out, wasn't at home, perhaps she was on her way back. Marcus let himself in, twisted the light, at least it was warm, round the clock heating, not too bright, dim. He liked his light dim, two leather travel bags by his side, a couple of duty-free bags in his grip. He pushed his luggage beneath the stairs into a crafted cupboard ridding himself of unnecessary clutter. He had hoped she would be waiting for him. He thought perhaps there might be a note lying around. He looked for signs, nothing of note. She kept herself well hidden, very enigmatic, part of the attraction.

The place appeared clean, had been designed that way, space, light airiness, she had taken good care of it in his absence. Absent for just over four weeks, he was a very busy man, big business, capitalising assets, maximising profits, ventures, adventures. He'd asked if she wanted to come out to visit. She said she couldn't possibly, the pressures of work, a noose around her neck. She said you know how it is and he had laughed.

Not enough time spent on her, he'd like to spend more on her. He'd brought back lots of presents. She'd like that.

In the taxi from the airport he thought about her, she crossed his mind and stopped midway perched on his third eye, top of his nose, little Bond girl, target victim, he loved that movie, oo Heaven and he thought perhaps she might be waiting for him and they could have a shower together.

Cold tiles on bare feet, shudder through his spine, old bones crack, crick. Marcus looked young for his age, young for those fifty summers, head full of hair, hay, hey that's not bad for a man his age. Fake tanned glow, still muscular, gym trim, drip, drop. . .

The force of the water invigorating his tired skin, refreshing, revitalising, remembering . . . dirty thoughts, rub a dub dub . . . flannelled away, eyes closed beneath a shower nozzle. He had looked forward to sharing a shower with her.

Flight grime washed off, soap cream swirling, froth sucked down a plug hole, steamed-up frosted glass, water shattering, splattering down on him.

Marcus scrubbed clean, tired, hungry.

The fridge was empty, disappointingly so, she could at least have filled it up.

Still alone and he ordered in some food. Poured himself a glass of ice cold water, cleansed his palate clean.

Clean outside, inside. And he waited.

The clock chimed ticking slowly on. He was ageing by the minute, she was making him wait and he didn't like that.

He telephoned his wife in the interim.

'Jane, it's Marcus.'

'Marcus where are you?'

'London.'

'Did you have a good flight?'

'Delayed for a while.'

'How are you?'

'Tired. And you?'

'With Gilly, we are getting piddled on wine, I'm afraid I've been a bad girl, been digging away at your little passion.' Jane was in good spirits, helping herself to his vintage wines. Marcus didn't mind, he was glad she was enjoying herself, happy Gilly was with her.

'How is Gilly?'

'Fine, Gilly's marvellous.' Jane's voice swooped to a dramatic whisper. 'Awful, poor thing's in a terrible way.'

Marvellous Gilly was having a rough time, indebted to her husband. In one stroke, her husband's stroke, poor Gilly had been left in the lurch. A final lurch over a sweet young boy. Mr Gilly's concluding farewell. House sold, liquidated, life insurance not worth the paper it was written on, thirty years of . . . had it really been that long? . . . charity lunches and all of a sudden Gilly had to go out and work for a living.

'Has she got a new man in her life?'

'Marcus don't be cruel.'

'I'm not being cruel. Tell Gilly I'll look after her.' Jane relayed the good news.

'Oh Marcus you are sweet,' came a high-pitched Gilly from the background. 'Here's to Marcus, three cheers for Marcus.'

'She sounds rather the worse for wear.'

'More trouble. Richard's in trouble.'

'Who?'

'Her godson, we saw him in . . .'

Marcus couldn't remember. 'How much trouble?'

'Lots and lots.'

'Lots and lots of wine, more wine, tell Marcus he's a saint,' shouted Gilly.

'Marcus you're being beatified. Do you hear?' and Jane giggled.

'I'll be back at the weekend. We can talk then.'

'Do you hear that Gilly . . . Marcus is arriving at the weekend and then we shall be saved.'

'Here's to good old Marcus.'

'Jane . . .'

'Yes?'

'Have a good evening, be kind to Gilly.'

Electronic kisses blown down a cable, whisked miles away, distance obliterated, words, noises, sounds travelling at the speed of light or faster and faster, time's fool, linked by a wire, misheard, mishmash, cross lines and if the system should fail, should come to a halt in one stroke, an exploding din . . .

the noise of the doorbell, shrill.

Din . . . dinner.

Sushi delivered, champagne bottle of, mineral water two bottles of, fifty quid, now you see it now you don't. An exchange of pleasantries with the young man hidden in his helmet, happy with his tip from the nice rich man, in his nice abode. He heard the happy revv of a motorcycle and off the young man rode.

Marcus was getting agitated, his stomach rumbled, Jane piddling to the back of his mind and she really should have been here for him. Sushi in a plastic woven basket getting warmer by the second. She was late, too late to eat together.

Marcus would start without her, she wouldn't mind, he should start without her. The plain brown paper bag emptied, mineral water opened, clean crockery, clean food, a bottle of champagne placed in the fridge. Sushi light, easily digested.

She should have let him know. He could have gone out, should have gone to his club. Restless. He'd left a message on the answerphone, he'd spoken to her only the day before, had offered to buy her a mobile phone, she resisted with delightful acts of independence.

Anytime, anyplace, anywhere, no, no . . . she said.

She said she would feel like a Martini girl, at the end of a line, tethered.

'Then Marcus I shall be completely within reach. Hardly enigmatic.'

She was funny sometimes. Charming, she made him laugh, funny ways and habits, lacking in foulness, quite unspoiled. It occurred to him she didn't seem to want anything from him. So naive.

'My emerald eyelight.' And she had scoffed aloud at his romantic effort. 'No one's ever called me that.'

His green-eyed mocker and he liked to see them shine, yearning, learning, all the time learning, inquisitive and happy. Refreshing to have youth staring up at you. Tiny thing, birdlike creature, quite beautiful in a waif-like way. A residue of childishness had anchored her to him.

Marcus believed in love, believed he loved her. Sometimes he wanted to squeeze her hard, make sure it wasn't an illusion, that she was there for him, that he had her. Not for ever but for the present. He could ponder on her for hours.

A present for his autumn years. Colour his autumn landscape bright.

He offered her respite.

'Why don't you study some more? Take a course in something.'

'Like what?'

'Whatever, I'll take care of the fees.'

'No thanks. All the same it's kind but, no it's not right.'

He thought he made her happy.

'Anything, I'll get you anything.'

'It's OK,' and she had sighed. 'Tell me about the time you were in India on a mission with the Buddhists saving black babies.'

She would sink into the large divan and open a magazine, pretend she wasn't listening.

He heard the key in the door, the key turning and in she walked.

Big fur hat on her, he had bought it in Paris for her, big high boots, he bought her those in New York. Long fur jacket, shabby worn out, a present from somebody else no doubt. A long time ago, it didn't matter, it was in the past.

Marcus made a mental note to buy her a new one. They would go shopping tomorrow. He would walk along New Bond Street in and out of the pretty shops with his pretty one by his side . . .

'Marcus . . . Marcus . . . sorry I'm late . . . it's freezing out there.'

Her face was red from the cold, it looked as if she had been crying.

Unwrapping herself from her outside attire she scurried over to him, planted a kiss upon his lips.

'Brrr.' Cold kiss, quick kiss, whiff of winter. 'Brrr.'

'Where were you?' He had a right to know, he was beginning to get worried.

'Camden, hanging out with the bums.'

She was in a bad mood.

'Good flight?' she asked, peering in the sushi container. Marcus said nothing.

She wasn't listening. 'Good . . . ooh good, sushi.'

'There's some sushi. I thought you might be hungry.'

'Have a good flight?' she called out from the downstairs bathroom.

He heard a sigh of relief, heard the trickle of her water splish splash the toilet basin, relieving herself. He thought he heard her sigh again, mutter a curse, her rosebud foul mouth, the chain flush, the faucet turned on, a dash of water streaked across her face.

She returned and sank into the sofa.

'Help me with my boots, Marcus,' she demanded and he did. 'Now tell me all, I want to know everything,' she squeezed his arm and snuggled into him. 'Everything, everything, I couldn't bear not being with you.' And she picked a magazine up from the glass topped, ashwood, designer coffee table. His coffee table, and she started flicking through it.

Marcus was looking at her, wondering.

'Really?' he asked.

She really wasn't paying adequate attention. His expectations left unconquered, he was going to have to say something, not more than a string of words but enough to bring her to heel. It would be nice if she had been there for him.

She wasn't listening.

'Well Marcus how was the flight?'

Rich pickings

Everything had gone pear shaped. Bea shaped. Brian was at his desk, lost in B-rated reveries, as in permissible thoughts he could have which Bea would approve of when –

'You are so repulsive,' bellowed Brian's boss.

She had caught him unconsciously picking his nose, a grey greener delicately hanging off the second digit of his right hand.

He had been trying to work out why Bea blamed him for Graham's outrageous behaviour at the dinner party. It wasn't like he'd instigated the thing but Bea kept hassling him about it. It had just been a laugh, a bet made in jest, he didn't actually believe Graham would pull it off. Twenty-five quid said he wouldn't, especially taking into consideration Graham had yet to meet Ruth but Graham desperate for a shag said looks didn't matter, upped the stakes to double or quits by deciding to play the dastardly bastard, a known method of seduction, inverse like, he assured Brian it never failed. Thus armed with enough alcohol to ensure obliteration and following a sumptuous feast of beans, insults, pulses and patronising putdowns, Brian and Bea disappeared into the kitchen to do the washing up and the next thing they hear is this grunting thumping coming from upstairs. Brian was creasing himself and Bea insisted on being let in on the joke, but she didn't get it.

Then Graham reappeared demanded payment and left. Worst of all was Ruth, who had stood at the door, waving him off, flushed faced and gushing,

'Are you sure you don't want to stay?'

Gobsmacked Bea was, her jaw hinge fixed so that all she could do was wag her finger beneath Brian's nose. Later she managed to articulate the phrase 'lowdown and cruel'.

Brian tried to level with her, Ruth was happy, Graham was happy, where was the harm, but she took the moral high ground and declared it an act of premeditated callousness.

Little Miss High and Mighty was beginning to get on his wick.

Pick wick chiding and Brian was intercepted for a second time by a hand holding out a tissue, his fair cheeks reddened. His attempt to destroy the evidence by smearing it along the underside of his desk had been foiled.

Brian winced, cheers, snatched the tissue and tried to ignore his chastising boss.

'What would your mother say?'

'My mother's dead.'

'Oh, oh, I'm sorry Brian.' And she swiftly exited.

Brian's mother had had a thing about keeping his nose clean. She would pick it for him as a boy. Clasp his nostrils between her fingers and tell him to blow hard. Sniffers were sniffed at, snivellers abhorred, sneezers and snotrag worn weepy snufflers despised, keep your nose clean boy and you'll get along grand. His nostrils were always crystal clear. No crusties allowed in the Martin household and it did her heart good to see him well turned out, spruced up and shiny faced.

He wondered what his mother would have made of Bea. His mother had warned Brian of women's scheming minds and wily ways. Make sure you find someone good, who'll look after you proper. A decent woman, like . . . well, like herself. His mother had never fully approved of Brian's past girlfriends least of all Julia. She tried not to show it but it was obvious, Julia's airs and graces had not been to her liking,

'A bit full of herself and her tone of voice Brian, too nasal.'

Though dead, Brian's mother had reincarnated in his conscience. She was with him all the way. Her voice clear as day, diluted Irish-English, just like himself. Brian's mother had been Irish, his father English. She had come from Galway and every summer the Martin family would take the ferry from Holyhead and drive across the country to Galway Bay. She'd come to England to work as a nurse, fell in love with Brian's father and stayed. Ordinary folk, they were just ordinary folk, her hair was black like his own, ah and she had blamed the Spanish swaggarts, the lost Armada crew. That's where Brian got his good looks from, she said it wasn't from his father's side of the family, that lot she said were ugly as sin, no his good looks were her doing. All his good points came from her side and that was that. She talked endlessly about home, but she never went back: 'Sure my life is here now, Brian.'

The sense being Brian was her life.

Mrs Martin had been dying of an incurable disease though this was only diagnosed at the post-mortem. On a winter afternoon on her way back from the butcher's and suffering from a bizarre strain of influenza, she had bent down to retrieve her handkerchief from off the kerb when a kid on a skateboard butt-butted her, hurtling the woman forward on to the street and underneath the wheels of a silver MG. A silver uninsured MG and the driver with a lust for life and freedom had slammed his foot on the accelerator. The driver was never traced, the kid was really shook up and everyone agreed it was a bloody disgrace that a woman of Mrs Martin's calibre should die in such a ludicrous manner. It made front-page news in the *Gazette* and the local council passed a by-law forbidding skateboarders on public pathways.

In the funeral parlour Brian and his father had sat by the open casket watching people come to pay their last respects. The creases had fallen from her face and Brian hadn't noticed before how lined she'd been. His father had chosen the outfit in which she lay resting, a knitted suit, something she'd have worn to mass, she liked to look smart. She would have wanted to look appropriate, it's not every day you get to meet your maker. Brian worried the suit didn't do much for her complexion. He'd suggested a deep burgundy twin set, a plaid skirt, cream shirt and matching jacket. But his father insisted she'd be much more comfortable in something softer.

Brian couldn't recall their last conversation and it bothered him. He had been busy up in London living with Julia being busy, sometimes Julia would forget to pass on the message that his mother had rung. He hated Julia for that.

Casket kiss before they shut her away. The casket closed

67

and heavy on his death-heavy shoulders, for she'd been a big woman, Brian carried her to the graveside.

In the wake of the burial, friends and family came back to the house and Brian had taken their coats up to his parents' bedroom, to lay them across the double bed. Her bits and pieces still warm still there. He had opened the wardrobe and was looking at her clothes unfolding her garments and sniffing, trying to memorise her scent. He'd left the door open and Adam wandered in, a polite cough to announce his arrival.

In Brian's hand a rumpled silk shirt, the one she used to wear on grand occasions for Christmas and the like. Rumpled and sodden, tear crushed and saddened.

Grief.

Women and grief. They had a habit of going hand in hand.

Bea was getting a bit too generous on dishing out the stuff and it felt to Brian like she was trying to invade his head, get inside his thoughts.

The problem being her unceasing questioning, like she was digging away at him, hoping to unearth some major piece of inconsequential grit so that she could flare up at him about it. The latest had been an unduly excessive mouthful received whilst walking along the South Bank. He had only been looking, there was no harm in looking, it wasn't as if he was leering or ogling: he was, as he put his case firmly and calmly forward, merely looking. The thing was and this was what really got to him the woman who had caught his attention wasn't even real, it was a billboard campaign. In your face merely two dimensional.

'That's not the point, Brian.'

He would not be made feel guilty about something so trivial.

What did Bea want?

That he be blinkered?

What was he to do?

Turn a blind eye?

Double affirmative.

'Brian it's not what you do, it's the way that you do it.'

Besides women liked to be looked at and he didn't mind if she looked at other guys. Bea was being ridiculous and there's a limit to how much a man can take, he would have to say something, soon. And yet, and yet in some warped way Brian enjoyed Bea's little insecurities, it made him feel bolder than he actually was.

Unconsciously his finger slipped back up a nostril.

He'd told Bea straight:

It's a boy thing, OK Bea?

It's a boy thing.

The Fantasy Bus

8.45 a.m.

Girl marches towards exit

Glowing with pig sweat courtesy of London Underground

Her weekly two-zone pass, inserted

Is spat out

Is retrieved

Is pushed back into a tatty red plastic holder over really gross
picture.

Girl wears a tight grey skirt and floral shirt, under a seasonal 3/4-
length jacket

She picks up a paper

Searches for change at the bottom of her bag

And her brain clocks into gear, begins to focus on the day ahead

Day a head

Keep it above water

She raises her eyes, searches for a break in the clouds

Cold windy morning cuts to the bone

'C'mon luv,' but it's monotonous grey at the bottom of her bag

And the paper is replaced

Clickity clack heels upon pavement

Short skirt strides shortened

Face frozen, nearing destination

And Girl crosses a wide busy thoroughfare

Approaches a stark concrete building on the right side of the

Thames
Standing to attention next to Her Majesty's knick-knacks
Kept under wraps by birds and blokes in fancy dress
9 a.m.
Girl walks through a large beckoning set of smoked glass doors
Throws her jacket on the back of a chair
Is drawn to the coffee machine
Coffee is percolated, black, settles in a plastic cup
Girl takes up appointed position, settles in a plastic chair
She puts on a face.
A smile from ear to ear
Sincere
Good morning X
Good morning
Why . . . well a lot of water has passed under the bridge
So Girl stationed at said location, temporarily
She will have you know, it's only temporary
Due to the death of the usual employee,
who slipped into a coma as she sat behind the desk
The post-mortem declared it was death by boredom
Her brain cells had gradually wittered away
Her head was empty when they opened her up.
Girl takes to tapping her fingers on the desk
Duties consist of sitting with a smile on her face
Harder than you may think, so you mustn't. Think.
Guests are required to sign in when entering and sign out when
    leaving
A task of much responsibility assigned to security guards who take
    it in shifts to sit beside Girl throughout the day
On this fine morning Arnold, a Northern racist homophobic
(Not his fault, environment in which he grew up)
With a heart of gold sits with Girl and keeps her company
9.30.

The morning rush subsides and strange
A slow bus trundles along the road
Strange it is painted blue
It is noticed and eyes are averted from papers, screens and coffee
     machines, office seats and bosses' cheeks . . .
And *oh là là* . . .
The big blue open top bus comes to a stop outside Girl's glass
     doors
Drum rolls and a cough to clear the maestro's throat
Ladies and Gentlemen behold the beautiful, the sensual, erotic,
     exotic member inflators, top titillators, visual masturbators

But I'm running ahead of myself.
On top of the bus stood in T-shirts and cowboy boots
Stood upright and outright in the cold morning air
They may catch their death of cold, perils of the job

Ladies and Gentlemen, three very lovely lassies
Fun gals come to brighten up our day
And the maestro pinched a proffered bum
Cheeky
'Come, take a closer look –
See'
Caught on camera by the TV crew
'Looksy, we know you want to.'
Hurrah, hurrah,
Hurry or you'll miss the show.
Girl gets distracted and red-blooded Arnold has already fled
She goes to have a decker
It's not every day you get to sample the best of British journalism
3 TITTY LADIES BARE ALL IN CITY WHOPPER SHOCKER
Smoked glass doors are opened wide
Girl and Arnold step outside
'Woah she's a ride,' says Arnold to Girl

'Go on gorgeous give us a twirl.'
'Awight boys,' calls out Titty One. 'We sure gonna have a load a
    fun.'
And slowly and ohh so teasingly
She pulls her T-shirt up over her body, revealing her . . .
And the crowd yell
'Cor look at the knockers on that.'
Tasty, tasty, very very tasty and tastefully exhibited
The important bits hidden behind a golden bikini thingy
9.43.

A good crowd has gathered
Fun for all means men and Girl
She doesn't seem to notice, neither do they
Otherwise preoccupied with Titty One
Her hips and bra straps and her bum
Sway in opposing directions
Man calls out 'Get a move on . . . some of us got work to do.'
Titty One satisfies
Her great big boobies are espied
The bikini thingy cast aside
How dutifully displayed
Titty One is most refined
She shows them off like a good little girl
Like she's a good little girl
Flutters her eyes never done it before
Then switches to acting like a dirty whore
In tune, the bleating audience sing the all-time classic, 'Get your
    tits out for the boys'.
9.45.

And like vermin they appear out of nowhere
'Tools down' and headed for the spectacle
The crowd has grown like a pregnant woman

Lines of males at windows
Windows opened for the first time ever
Cheering and the like
Then Titty Two joins her pal
She really is a horny gal
'All for you' coos Titty Two,
'But don't tell the wife.' And she pouts out her tush wagging it like
    a puppy bitch
Standing naked without a stitch, on
'Could do with a piece of that.'
'Wouldn't know what to do.'
'Would too.'
Fisty cuffs are formed, punches thrown
'Boys, boys there's plenty for all,' says Titty Three
She lifts up her top, see, see
9.50.

An enormous blob of dribbly drool
Descends down the building forming a pool
Titties titillating tight trousered crowd and Girl taken in, goes
    along for the ride
She has become a part of the thronging mass
She's always been a strong-willed lass
Girl cheers those ladies on
'Whey, hey.'
Places two fingers in her mouth and lets out a screeching wolf
    whistle
Draws attention to herself
Camera swings into action
'Bravo, Ladies, bravo.'
Focus switches and Girl comes into view
Full frontal, fully clothed
9.52.

Males are disconcerted, don't know what to do
Very unbecoming behaviour
From a proper Lady.
Most unsettling and definitely not right
Girl should be behind her desk,
Out of sight
The men feel cheated
It's their show and they attack her with cries of
Lesbo lesbo and Girl shouts back,
'Would you blame me, look at the state of yous lot' and the Titties
    laugh
'Good on you Girl' they shout their support. 'Good on you Girl.'
Men lose face, bosses lose money and it's back to work boys
9.55.

The crowd disperses and the wheels on the bus go round and
    round, round and round.

Bea's fight

Bea was in the kitchen turning up the hob.
Brian was in the bathroom playing with his knob.
Graham was on the t/phone chattering to Bob
When dooowwnn flew a blackbird and . . .

Donald's was bigger.

Sizzling sausages on a Sunday morning, the pan doused in fat and Bea dressed in one of Brian's cast-offs. The wearing and sharing of one's lover's attire being a benefit of any decent relationship, and as Bea was currently in a very decent (and sexually fulfilling) relationship she took full advantage of this, although instinctively keeping a close eye on her knickers. It was an 'about the house' shirt, torn and washed out. Brian had dragged it from his pile of dirty washing and Bea could smell him off of it. A few extra splashes of grease wouldn't go amiss, she pierced the porker skin, watched the fat oozle out.

Sausages side by side, measuring up and every man Bea ever went out with had religiously requested confirmation on being the biggest entry, so amongst other things she masturbated their egos and lied.

Yeah Donald's was definitely bigger.

★

It was raining, suffice to say there was no better incentive to staying in than a swift glance outside to where the wet tumbled with purpose. A blurred view from the kitchen window of a sole mangy blackbird, dangling precariously on a washing line next to a ragged tea towel, presented the exact notion of how a holy sabbath should be spent, when all one aims to do is mong in front of the television set. Pure luxury to spend the day cuddled up in the arms of your loved one, singing along to musical scores and munching highly calorific food. Bea was hungover on love's syrup, nursing a satisfied dampness while Radio 1 played humalong, 'you know at least one line of the song' pop tunes. Stood by the sink rinsing tomatoes, ripe plum tomatoes, hard yet soft, veg or fruit, you win some, you lose some . . . they had called it quits, do you give up? yeah do you? . . . mmmmmmmmm.

Brian and Bea had made it through their first major row. It had been on the simmer for quite a while and was as fresh as the orange squeezed from the carton. A gathering of irritants had come to the boil, the possibility of losing Brian for ever evaporated and Bea could relax again a while. It had been touch and go, communication had ceased for a period of over sixteen hours. Sixteen hours of picking up the receiver and then 'on better thoughts' replacing it. Sixteen hours of inner slander, lip-biting fury and breast berating.

But it was all over now, all smoothed over, gone forgotten and handling it like a pro Bea made sure they were closer than ever.

Sure everybody fights, isn't it only part and parcel of being in a mature and loving relationship, isn't it only normal, well isn't it?

★

Frying sausages comparing men, oh she had learned a lot. Of course she was older now, more experienced, a woman of the world was what Bea considered herself to be. Things had changed. Bea was keeping notes, she was not going to make the same mistake twice.

The thing with Donald was, the prick had never really loved her, well not as she loved him. Bea had always been there for him, whenever, wherever, ever forgiving. The first time he shat on her she found out by chance. Picked up the extension receiver about to ring her mother for a moan, caught Donald talking to girl:

'So that's it,' he was saying.

'Yeah the drink got the better of me,' she replied.

Bea's heart thumped. Infuriated she was. Infuriated, knew the voice yet couldn't fit it to a face, where the hell was it coming from and who in God's name was . . . was . . . She shut up her thoughts, listened to Donald grovel.

'Can I see you again.'

'No,' came the reply. 'I don't think so.'

'I don't ask twice.'

'That's fine by me.'

'OK, so I'll be off then.'

'OK.'

'You're sure?'

Bea replaced the receiver about to belch her heart out, struck dumb, a wide ache in the pit of her stomach. Donald had been rejected and she felt a tinge of sorrow for him. Analysing the situation from her perspective she decided there was no point fretting, maybe nothing had happened, maybe she was jumping to conclusions, and maybe, just maybe the moon was a big cheese soufflé after all. Donald

78

was probably calling the girl's bluff, sure hadn't they only moved in together, hadn't they only just signed a six-month lease. Bea was going to let this one ride. The girl clearly wasn't interested, it would be all right, he had her. See, and she levelled with herself, Donald was a real man, and wasn't that what she wanted after the experience with Shay.

The rain splashed down making heavy-handed noises. Bea turned the sausages in the pan, then added quartered tomatoes.

She loved the sound of rain. It brought her back to the dampness of Dublin and the feeling of victory when you were inside, warm and dry. She had met Donald in Dublin, in the rain. He had been standing at the door of the Stag's Head forming an arch with one of his arms. A Gaelic sentinel verbally halting her passage inside.

'Where are you off to?' he asked.

'The bar, where d'you think?' and she pulled a retard face.

He laughed, 'Will you buy us a drink so?' and proffered her his empty pint glass by way of an introduction.

God he was such a charmer. She should have known then she was on to a loser. God she hadn't had a clue back then and it being a Sunday Bea muttered a quick prayer that this time, this time, things would work out.

Fry-ups banned at Ruth's meant Sundays were spent in Brian's on condition the kitchen was in a reasonable state to cook in. A 'reasonable state' being one of those phrases

79

which translate badly between the sexes and Bea found herself with a pair of rubber gloves on and a Brillo in her hand. She could have shouted at Brian, said there was no way she would cook in such filth but she stopped herself, rolled up her sleeves and got cracking. Treading carefully in the aftermath of the blow-up she reckoned there was no point in undoing all that hard work.

Of course there had been minor misunderstandings to date, a few testings of the boundaries but nothing of major importance. It wasn't that she was insecure, she just liked to know where she stood. Parameters were to be well and truly delineated, there would be no overstepping the mark. In the game of love Bea took no chances. Chance was akin to vulnerability and life's lessons had instructed her that vulnerability was a bum deal. She needed to know exactly what was going on in her partner's head, it wasn't a case of mistrust, more a desire to keep ahead of the competition. Those heady days of sweaty lust were on the decline. Her stomach no longer jingled whenever they met, her palms no longer clammy and her cheeks barely reddened when he stood naked beside her, limp.

Cracks became apparent, compromises were having to be made.

Brian's bad morning moods.

Bea's bad morning breath.

Questions asked like,

Where were you? . . . and who with?

Do you love me?

Are you sure?

How much?

Can you quantify it specifically?

Niggly bits were making themselves noticed.

One particularly horrible discovery had come to Bea's attention in the form of a trail of snots smeared along the wall beside the toilet. Her initial reaction was to blame Graham but the bathroom at Ruth's was wall flowering encrustations. Disgusted, she would clip them off with her nails. As for Brian he let it be known her insistent search and destroy campaign, to clear all blackheads from off his back, was highly irritating nor was he enamoured by her vocal capacity to belch loudly after meals and then feign surprise by politely excusing herself with a 'pardonnez moi'.

She had cottoned on to the latter, when all curried and beered up and laughing in the local Indian she bent towards Brian repeating their job titles with increasing speed and volume 'PA, PR, PA, PR, PA, PR, PA, PR, PA, PR, until finally releasing a small explosive vindaloo gust of 'ARPP'.

Brian didn't get it so she waved her hands in front of her mouth to create a waft. But he sat there stoic, then said 'Bea you're embarrassing yourself.'

In the column 'Things we have in common' Bea noted 'a mutual tendency to pick' and in the column 'Things not to do' she wrote 'stinking rassers'.

As far as Bea could objectively interpret the dispute in question: it was all his fault but she blamed herself. It began two weeks back after a Saturday shopping expedition ended abruptly and had gathered force up into the wee small hours of the night before.

Incident 1

Squeezing herself into a pair of size twelve jeans Bea was feeling especially trim when Brian remarked they looked too tight.

'What do mean tight, Brian? They're not tight, they're snug.' And she did an Anthea Turner.

'See, snug,' but they were visibly riding up her crack and Brian bored rigid having been in every high street shop twice and going through stacks of rails said unthinkingly and rather loudly,

'Bea, try on size fourteen.'

'Size fourteen, size fourteen, don't be ridiculous, I'm not size fourteen. It's the styling that's wrong on them, that's all,' says herself wondering if the material would stretch.

'Your boyfriend's right,' smarmed the assistant, 'you should stick to your proper size.'

'Don't say I didn't tell you,' added Brian and Bea went ballistic.

'Oh forget it, forget everything, Christ I hate shopping with you Brian, I hate it. You're just so unhelpful, so unhelpful. Worked a year as a sales assistant and you think you're ... you're a Christian ... Galliano or something.'

She rushed into the communal changing room, to an all-round view of herself and as she peeled the jeans back off her skin, she kept her eyes fixed on the carpet, no point in being a complete glutton for punishment.

Fuming internally Bea later asked Brian if he thought she was fat.

'Nah, just well proportioned.'

'Well proportioned my arse.'

'Especially your arse,' he sniggered and grabbing himself a handful of cheek he gave it a good old squeeze. Not surprisingly these were explosive words as far as Bea was concerned. She tugged at her lip and laughed it off, water off a duck's back, oil on water. Not very funny.

Incident 2

She was to meet Brian in a bar at seven, she told him to be on time, it was quarter past, she had only just arrived herself, he wasn't there. Twenty past seven and she went for a ten-minute saunter round the block. Half seven, OK maybe he was hiding in the corner somewhere, she looked about, no Brian and then escaped to the Ladies to powder her nose. Seven-forty and she was getting anxious, she was getting thirsty. She ordered a gin and tonic and stood by the bar, sipping slowly, wishing she had a paper to hide behind. The bar was packed, everyone could see her, stood up by the bar, stood up. Seven-fifty and she asked some guy for the correct time just in case her watch was slow. She said 'Do you have the time?' and he answered 'Sorry luv, I'm with my boyfriend.' Seven-fifty-five and she asked the barman the name of the bar just in case she had got the wrong place and he said 'You Irish crack me up.' Eight o'clock, an hour late and a flustered panting Brian came rushing through the door with an ironclad excuse. But Bea wasn't having any of it, she burst out crying and demanded to be taken home immediately.

Incident 3

At the Club, Bea hand locked to Brian who was chatting away to a media mate. She didn't know anyone and wasn't in the mood. Ian her boss was acting a right royal pain. He was stressed out with work, his numbers not quite adding up so he took it out on Bea, took her up on any little error even when it was blatantly his. She had hoped for a quiet evening of offloading but Brian said it would cheer her up to get out for a bit. And then there she was surrounded by lots of cutesy girls, all size eights, half-pints, must be starving themselves to death, it's not natural. Anorexia nervosa was making *her* nervous and Brian wasn't listening, Brian's eyes were on a wander. To top it off she overheard him mutter to a mate, 'Whoa babe alert,' and she obviously wasn't included. She found it impossible not to notice Brian's extracurricular glances and though she told herself not to be possessive, her guts twisted whenever she caught him on the leer. Brian had a subtlety problem, apt to come over all primitive on sighting a shapely female and burst into vocal grunts. Common sense recommended she bite her lip and not be making a scene, one dirty look does not deserve another when the latter would be interpreted as the neurotic female type.

'Mustn't be jealous,' thought Bea, 'must not be jealous. Don't go getting irrational girl. It's you he wants, loves, is with' she was desperate to convince herself.

. . . then

Incident 4

Determined to diet or at least to try it, Bea was filling her supermarket basket with lowfat, slimline products when a tempting banoffee pie caught her eye and she stalled for a moment deliberating whether or not she could allow herself a treat. Whilst Bea was entranced a tall thin woman had marched up the aisle and planted kisses on either side of

Brian's face.

'Brian darling, long time.'

What's more they spoke very familiarly for a further ten minutes and didn't include her.

'So who's Jay?' asked an aggravated Bea.

'Great woman, we used to work together, she runs her own production company now.'

'Oh yeah' – and Bea wondered what exactly did Brian get up to when they weren't together, he was probably all over anything that moved, probably threw himself at their feet . . . mustn't get jealous, must not get jealous, don't go getting irrational girl.

'Known her long, have you?' queried Bea.

Damn it but she had a right to know of everything BBC . . . Before Bea Chrissakes, Brian's past, as far as she was concerned fell within her scope of control.

'Jay? Yeah we go back a long way.'

Do you now and Bea demanded just how far. She had to get it out of her system, she had to make him feel small and insecure, so she showed him the remains of his handiwork on Ruth's bathroom tiles.

'Jesus Brian isn't this disgusting? Ruth says it wasn't her but who else could it be?'

Mortally embarrassed he was, didn't like that at all, not at all so to get back at her . . .

Incident 5

An answerphone message announced Brian was going out with the lads. All very well but Bea was furious. She assumed they would be going out together as they normally did every

85

Friday night. The friggin' little shizzer, the git would you warrant it, could he not have rung her at work, given her some kind of notice. Given time she too could have made arrangements. But now, now she would have to spend the whole evening in watching TV with Ruth. So she goes home thinking she'll make the best of it. A girls' night in and Ruth has the audacity to be out as well. The first time Ruth of the no social life, no personality, no nothing variety was not at home. The where and how of it had Bea perplexed. It turned out Ruth had gone up the West End giving out food to the poor and needy which in truth was a friend-finding mission. She arrived back at eleven pretty shook up and nursing a black eye, hadn't some drunken alco only gone and thrown a swipe at her.

'It was awful Bea, terrible to see people living like that, terrible.'

'So what did you do?'

'I gave him everything I had, I mean I had to, it's so wrong that some people have so much and others so little.'

'Ruth he'll probably just spend it on booze.'

'I didn't exactly have a choice, Bea.'

One swipe was enough for Ruth and the clenched fist threatening to do her in unless she gave him all her money was a further hint. She'd dropped her bag and run.

'Well if it makes you feel any better I've had a shit night too,' and Bea started telling Ruth about Brian.

Then who should arrive on her doorstep, 4 a.m., drunk and horny.

'Bea, my darling Bea.'

Bea icy cold.

'Had a good evening then?'

'Yeah great.' With drunken nerve Brian described how

they had wandered from bar to club to bar, how it was the best night out he'd had in ages. How . . . and Bea said 'Did you not think of ringing earlier so like I could arrange something.'

'But it just came up.'

'So what do you want?'

'I want to come in.' She winced at his puppy expression and slammed the door in his face. He rang the bell for ages even rang her up on his mobile phone. She told him where to go, he got stroppy and through the letterbox she yelled,

'Go fuck yourself Brian Martin.'

Ruth lurking in the background stepped out of the shadows and urged Bea to be sensible, to let him in before the neighbours complained. Bea stood her ground so Ruth made up a bed on the sofa and Brian slept on it.

The next morning the sofa was empty. Bea thought he had gone to the shops to buy her a bunch of flowers and beg forgiveness for being so thoughtless. So she waited in, and she waited all day. No sign of Brian, not even a call. Sixteen hours later beside herself with grief, she rang him. He received her coolly, asked if she had calmed down. She said she was sorry and needed to see him. Knackered after the previous night's excesses, Brian wanted to chill. Bea doubly peeved at the prospect of an ultra-boring weekend persuaded him to take her to the cinema, promising not to get annoyed if he fell asleep during the film.

But he didn't fall asleep, the leading lady was gorgeous and naked, the leading man nothing to write home about and totally clothed throughout.

As the credits rolled Brian remarked 'Great actress', and Bea thought he was so full of shit.

'No Brian, what you mean is great body,' which was true 'cause the actress hardly said anything.

'Ohh jealous are we,' snarled Brian.

'Don't be so stupid.'

He put his arm around her.

'She's not a patch on you.'

Lies, lies damnable lies, if only she could believe him.

'Liar.'

'Look, you were the one who wanted to go to the cinema.'

Final incident – bringing things to a head

Bea's back was got up, Brian's back was got up and nothing was said till safely back indoors. Nothing spoken till into bed they got.

And another thing . . .

What? . . .

Brian trying it on anyway.

And another thing . . .

WHAT?

I don't feel like it tonight . . .

Great.

Silence.

The side light switched off and verbal attacks travelled, they were bitching at each other, a swift jibe here, a cutting thrust there, each on the attack. Voices raised, hushed, raised, hushed, semi-joking insults dashing back and forth, tossed over the eiderdown and then Brian goes and says that in Ethiopia women can make their men come by just sitting on them.

'What do you mean?'

'You know, clenching and unclenching.'

'Are you saying I'm loose.'

Chrissakes it had only been in the last ten years that Bea had come to terms with having a clitoris, the last six on how to use it and now she had to go and be doing internal exercises. It was all too much for Bea.

'You're no King Dong yourself, titch.'

Bea had gone for the jugular. Knocked Brian sideways and he turned his back to her in a major huff.

That last punch came from nowhere, got him where it hurt, eh?

'Size is not important,' and Brian the Basher was dragged from the ring, his fans seething. For a while it looked like it would go the other way but wait . . . here's Bea Bust-a-Gut . . . hey victorious champion how are you feeling?

'Well a bit guilty actually, maybe I shouldn't have been so hard on him. I was always confident I had the upper hand it was just a matter of timing, maybe I shouldn't have been so merciless.'

Master of the Sulk was ignoring her now, it had a lot to do with being an only child. Bea more explosive could feel her anger subsiding and wanted to make up. Donald used to walk out, walk for days, slam the door with a 'Fuck you, you give me a headache.' Bea couldn't stand that, not knowing where she stood. She used to sit in their flat blubbering 'I don't know how to looooooooovvvvvveeeee him' like a right Magdalena.

Channels of communications must be kept open, whatever the cost.

'Brian.'

'Brian . . .'

'Br . . . ia . . . n,' whined Bea.

Oh blow it and she bandaged the first skirmish by going down.

Men can be so sensitive, she told him he had the biggest weenie peenie in the universe.

And he believed her.

From the bathroom she could hear Brian singing.

'Do you want tea or coffee?' she shouted out to him from the kitchen.

Mushrooms, tomatoes, rashers, fried egg, toast, sausages and a nice cup of tea. They had hardly slept, boy . . . had they made up or what.

She switched on the kettle, took out the forks and knives, plates and mugs. Almost there and she put three tea bags in the scalded pot. She had made enough for the three of them, included Graham 'cause he had accompanied her to the shops and paid for all the stuff.

Six eggs cracked in the pan, all perfect, yolks intact. She was glad they had made up, Brian and herself had a lot going for them.

Yesirree Mr Martin I'm thinking I'm feeling a lot for you.
Plenty of grease, the eggs turned easily, sunny side up.

'Ready,' she called.

A smell of aftershave followed by Brian, who had crept up
behind her and kissed her lightly on the neck.

'Looks great, Bea.'

She flicked the ladle to shoo him out of her way, filled
each plate and took a pile of buttered toast from the warm
oven.

She loved playing mammy.

'Here you go,' and she laid their plates in front of the TV
set, yeah she loved playing mam, come to think of it she was
also partial to a bit of doctors and nurses.

With hindsight and in the local gym doing an aerobics class,
Bea's head bent down between her legs, she came to the
realisation that Brian and herself had reached stage two of her
relationship calculations.

Bea philosophical thought dictated relationships were
tripartite: the 'wet patch' representing the initial period of
discovery, i.e. lots of sex, is then followed by the 'rough
patch', a time when the couple try and mould themselves
together into a whole unit, i.e. lots of fights which hopefully
(fingers crossed, praise the Lord and don't be walking under
ladders) brings the couple closer together ready for the final
stage, the 'dry patch', i.e. survival of the fittest whereby in
nine out of ten case studies the couple get married.

It really is that simple.

However the rough patch is notoriously dangerous and
straightening up, arms stretched over her head, the blood

rushing from Bea's face, she was aware that she now knew just as much about Brian as she was ever going to find out. Meant the rest would invariably be either padding or lies. Meant honesty would begin to fade and knowledge would have to be gained by some force of conniving extraction.

Concluding she would have to keep a tight hold on the situation and double her efforts in monitoring their progress, Bea plunged her head back down between her legs with reinforced vigour and caught a topsy-turvy view of a world in motion, jogging.

Cut & dried

The dregs of winter clinging, nose tip cold and running and with a smoke-heavy headache hanging on his right temple, Adam coughed.

His mouth widened and out spat a winter droplet, expelled from his body, hurtling through the air to fall, and by the wayside he spotted a budding crocus in a wet dew garden, a purple stem sticking upright, perpendicular.

The first sighting of natural colour to emerge from a city grey.

Organic pigment, no purer beauty. Its cracked earth rising journey, dirty soiled beginnings, standing impertinent before the elements. A delicate destiny unfolding, to be clumsily picked or trampled beneath a shoddy boot or perhaps disappear underground, to bulb out.

Pure purple. Yellow too and white, yellow on the way. Daffodil stems rising like the sun, flower rodents if you let them.

The season changes and the earth opens up to spill out its colour.

Nothing's ever black and white.

★

Work headed, station walking Adam's case load fell heavy on his mind. His leather briefcase swinging in step with leather upper soles. He coughed again, his body morning waking. He had assumed the CPS would drop the case but it made good reading, kept Joe Public's eye on the front page. No doubting but the dirt was being raked, no stone left unturned. Foreseen as a foregone conclusion.

Cut and dried.

And it was left to Adam to moisten it up.

Meetings were held, privileged conversations had, to determine CC's state of mind, to determine it was all in 'her' head.

CC and 'herself' had been seen drinking after a show in the theatre's green-room. *Tête-à-tête* flirtations, a drunken discourse ending in discord. She had stormed off. CC said she flew off the handle. And following to placate her, CC had, well this is what he claimed, placated her.

Pig legs dangle in Spanish taverns, cut and dried salted meat, chewed upon hard to moisten up. Spain, one late summer, Adam, Hayley, Ben and after graduation, after the wedding, they had taken to the roads in a pale blue battered Morris Minor. He remembered driving into Madrid, Hayley with a map across her lap, plotting the route, her tanned elbow resting on the lowered window. Ben asleep in the back. Flies stuck to the screen, fell like rain against his window shield, felled by wiper swords. Country roads grew to a six-lane motorway. It had crept up on them, Madrid visible, eighty miles per hour in a clapped-out car. In the middle of the road, vehicles either side, dancing in the aisles, zipping from one lane to another. Adam's eyes fixed in front and Hayley had turned her outward gaze inward, looked directly at him, understood everything about him. She was smiling at his concentration, she had made him laugh. Disturbed his train of thought.

A carriage of cold sped underground. An underground assembly of commuting germs, a communal gathering of viruses colouring the air. Adam reached into his pocket retrieved a packet of bright orange lozenges, popped the foil and popped the lozenge into his mouth. He was lucky, he had a seat.

He had a paper and he began to read.

His friends had warned him, told him he was losing it. You're mad, mad, you don't want to bring up another man's child. It wasn't like that, he was perfectly sane, in love. Insanely in love. Hayley was ten years his senior, a decade of distance between them. He had never met a woman quite like her before. She held his heart in her hands and squeezed hard.

It had taken eight years to come undone, five of them married, five of them happy. Then and then, something grew between them, forcing them apart.

At arm's length they viewed their respective lives and yearned for change. Hayley was offered a prominent position on the other side of the world and Adam awarded a partnership in a very reputable law firm. Clever enough to acknowledge doomed love and another fucked-up kid, they redirected themselves. It was all very amicable, terribly mature.

Terrible.

Time to move on, move forward.

His friends, ever eager to entice him, did their best to

match Adam up, to fill that extra space. Two years without a woman, it just wasn't normal; none the less he played the game and pretended to be interested. A continuing spate of blindingly boring dates. Evenings spent opposite intense thirty-year-old women yearning for someone to father their future children, prematurely flushed in fear of the ominous shelf. Courteously Adam applied dampened handkerchiefs to their brows but would go no lower. Numerous coffees declined for the sake of his sanity.

Initially left in his emptiness, he'd molusced a while, let the dust settle till the sharp edges smoothed over. Had felt an oncoming break so he took himself to New York to visit an old friend.

An engine brew of heat, the first thing to hit, then lazy accents, passport control and, 'Hey Adam, good to see you.' Tom was waving to him from the arrivals pen.

Fast forward over the past and a couple of beers further down the line they had found their rhythm again, their boy beat, scandal stories and do you remember the time we . . .

Followed by ten days of making memories, of yellow cabs and cocaine-kindled 'tauc', clubs, bars, you want it, they got it and it amounted to a pile of receipts. A stack of bills wedged in Adam's wallet to reassure himself he was having a good time. Tom playing the pied piper and he was eager to lead Adam astray, to show Adam what a wonderfully wild life he was having. So one night for a bit of light entertainment Tom ordered in some company. They had a laugh, these were smart women, good at what they did, unafraid to take control of the physical challenge.

'So what did you think?' asked Tom to his novice.

'Instantly gratifying but . . .'

'But?'

'No aftertaste.'

'Shit man you've such high ideals.'

'Nah I just yearn for an aftertaste.'

The first night of Cambridge, face down the porcelain, initiating themselves in the perils of vodka. They had met back in the days of diced carrots, had shared the same landing. 'Hi, I'm Tom and I'm . . . I'm an American.'

In college life had been different, altruistic. Hours spent pondering, articulating thoughts. Cerebrally impassioned when there were no stakes at all, when the blurring of boundaries seems to make sense.

CC had been getting a bit tetchy of late, a bit apprehensive regarding the night in question. He'd been culled, had been well oiled and unable to remember details, it had all blurred slightly out of focus.

Cut and dried.

Adam had chewed upon his situation and hardened up.

See it's easier when everything is paid for up front. In control you know where you are. You got to keep on top of things, keep on going so like an ostrich Adam detoxed himself from feeling, buried his head in the deep damp sand and it began to make sense. No emotional outlay, no exchange of numbers, no mindfuck games, unless specifically requested and absolutely no consequences. Quids in, a form of self-protection.

Fine-comb questioning, Adam and CC had been over it a hundred times or more. He did his best to reassure CC, they would work it to their advantage. Fluid in the dark place and hardly any bruises, nothing that passion couldn't account for.

97

That a certain event had occurred was not in dispute, it was from what angle it could acceptably be perceived, the understanding of one's intentions, of interpreting signals. Word pitched against word, trying to make some sense out of it.

The evidence collected, collated, the case now in the process of discovery.

Adam coughed, a polite indication to show he was on the move. His stop, his paper refolded and under his arm. He crossed the gap.

The gap was closing.

CC had a vague feeling 'she' had done it before.

'She' had made some obscure reference which he couldn't quite remember.

CC was sure she had done it before.

CC said this, CC said that, a childhood copycat game. He said she had been screaming something about this time, this time she was going to do something, she wouldn't take shit from no one, no one was going to fuck her over this time.

She the whiter than white, the purer than pure was becoming discoloured, distasteful.

Adam and CC sieve, sifting through the finer points of the case.

'It's important. Try and recall as much detail as you can.'

On the RIP

OK I admit it, I take responsibility for my actions but really, what does one expect if put in a certain situation?

Freedom has its price and shackle free I was game.

I was all dollied up and in an uplifting mode Hello Boys, doe eyed, empty faced my eyelashes aflutter mouth partially open, butter pouting . . . touting See I'm well read and osmosis has taken its toll Sure wasn't I only doing what was expected Well a woman has certain needs, certain desires, fuck it my gaoler had flown the coop and left me the key to his heart.

Plaaaaytimmmme . . . and I turned to Bea to give me a helping hand. But Bea otherwise preoccupied has taken up the role of adjunct and become a Brian clone, unmotivated to do anything unless he's with her:

'Sorry I'm too tired.'

'Sorry I just want to stay in tonight.'

'I'm not really bothered, sorry.'

Falling in love means shitting on your friends well at least till the first major bust-up.

Fact was my social life had taken a major nosedive and I

had to find some temporary playmates, so I started being friendly with the girls at work.

And then out of the blue Bea calls and she assured me it was only a minor tiff.

'It was nothing really, honestly', it had all blown over and everything was back to normal. In fact better than ever, especially sex.

OOhhh and herself confided that she had started doing these exercises and would soon be able to have a continuous orgasm for ten minutes.

'Really,' I gasped. 'Mine usually last for at least half an hour.'

She went all quiet, seemed perplexed and I had to tell her I was winding her up.

Then mentioning that Brian had prearranged a night out with the lads she asked me if I fancied a girly one.

'Shucks Bea but I'm busy.'

'What are you doing?'

'Clubbing.'

'Clubbing?' and Bea was surprised, thought she was my only friend. 'Who with?'

'A girl called Marla.'

'Can I come?'

'No, we're on the pull. You don't want Brian getting jealous now do you?'

'Yeah you're right,' she says. 'Hadn't thought of that.'

I concede to being a tad fucked off by Bea virtually ignoring me. It's understandable in the first stage of a new relationship but four months down the line and my patience is waning. Bea has found a life which apparently single women don't fit into 'cause they are man-eaters and aren't they just.

★

I met Marla through work, a large firm of legal eagles called Spittle and Dribble Esqs, 'Sons of Sons of' who occupy a corner building and thus have the luxury of front receptionists and back receptionists. The girls working the front wear uniforms, have percolated coffee, sofas and decent papers. The girls (Marla and myself) working down the back, have workmen, tabloids and instant. We take care of deliveries, make sure everything is signed for and man a conveyor belt of calls for our masters above.

'Awight?' Marla was grinning at me. It is usual practice for regular staff to take a back seat and give us temps experience of hard work and muscles in our answering arms. Marla was flicking through the pages of the latest edition of *Hello!*

'Ow doesn't she look lovely,' and she pointed to a hideous picture of a pastel Queen Mum.

'I can't believe that woman still allows herself to be photographed, you'd think she'd retire from the public eye and die,' I snorted.

'Nahh she's lovely.' Marla's lilting cor blimey accent was grating on my nerves, such accents having the same effect as chalk shrieks down a blackboard.

'I'd love her for a nan, I would.' She smiled affectionately and rubbed her index finger up and down the photo.

Quite a woman was our Marla, what she lacked in the cerebral department she made up for elsewhere. Every penny Marla earned went on clothes or make-up, she even put a bit away each month towards a breast enhancement fund. Life without a Wonderbra was death. None the less she was a striking lass, 5 foot 11 and hair bleached blonde falling halfway down her back. Her legs were amazing, only God help her when she gives birth, being one of those women with expandable arses and oceanic hips. She made the most of her 9–5 life amassing an encyclopaedic knowledge of the not so private lives of minor media celebs but at the end of the day she was a good-time girl, either in yer face or on top of it.

She asked how long I'd been living in London. I lied, told her I'd arrived the week before, had no friends and was living in a bedsit in King's Cross.

'Ain't you got a man then?'

I lowered my eyes and did my best Bea.

'He left me,' I said. 'Found out he was sleeping with my best friend behind my back. We'd been together since college, we were going to get married, it was awful, awful.'

'Ow shameful, are you OK?' squeaked Marla sympathetically and she handed me a tissue. I blew my nose, nodded my head.

'Sure?'

'Certain.'

'They're all wankers,' she said trying to cheer me up and asked if I wanted to go clubbing on Saturday.

I said 'Yeah.'

I said, 'Marla let's hit the town,' and she got nervous. She hadn't really expected that.

Marla informed me exactly what she would be wearing so I wouldn't clash, even dragged me out for some late night shopping in the hope of persuading me into a purple number almost as big as its price tag. I didn't succumb but standing in front of my emptied wardrobe, my clothes heaped upon the floor, I was vexed by indecision. Eventually I settled on the semi-paedophile look, a tight kiddies T-shirt that crushed my breasts, emblazoned with a pair of red lips and the word Sucker written above (tailor made I thought, tailor made), a pair of shiny black velvet hipsters and high black strappy heels. My bellybutton played hide and seek depending on my movements and my hair gripped with kiddy slides was all tufty soft with strategic wisps falling about my face. I was looking fairly miaow wow – albeit a bit contrived.

We were to meet at Fargas, a cocktail bar in Covent Garden. I arrived half an hour late, Marla and her mates an hour. Appearing like a lighthouse to the lone lost skipper, she snaked through the bar in a yellow micro mini-hipster and see-through black top, turning heads with six-inch heels and wired double Ds. She had a replica on either side of her, one called Rachel, the other Sharon, and we exchanged Awights.

Sharon worked as a receptionist at the last place Marla had worked and was studying aromatherapy. Rachel was a hairdresser but wanted to be a dancer.

'Watcha,' screeched Marla killing off a thousand cilia in one go.

'I got to hand it to you Marla, you look absolutely stunning.' She wiggled her ass by way of response. So subtle, so sublimely subtle.

'You look fab too, bet you'll make a killing tonight.'

'Hope so,' said I honestly.

We were outside the club standing behind a steel barrier awaiting inspection, our worthiness to be determined by the fascist bitch on the door. The girl with the list. The almighty list for the really cool. We were merely the cold and there was a sharp north wind licking about us. 'I'd love to be a girl on the door,' simpered Rachel. 'It's so sophisticated, so glamorous.' Marla chatted to one of the bouncers to ease our passage, though we had arrived early enough to guarantee entrance. Early enough to nab a table and ensconce ourselves there, lay out our belongings to mark our territory.

The club was vibrating, all lights and darkness, the music thumping. Chrome, metal, mirrors. Everything deliberately pieced together for the desired vibe. Everyone vying for attention. Men and women taking up their prescribed positions. Girls writhing on the dance floor in an effort to enchant or crowding out the toilets in an effort to enhance. Guys stood by the bar leeching or doing the circuit, picking out the wheat from the chaff, the cream of the crop. It was quite a social club, not as serious as some places where the music is the main attraction, where one goes to nod one's head, nor was it a complete pickup joint, oozing with sleaze. It strikes a happy medium. It strikes the midnight hour. The bewitching hour was upon us and I wondered if I'd succeed.

I was hankering after a conquest, nudge, wink, know what I mean, a bit of rump to bump off. I relished the thought, my tongue tingled, my pulse pulsated in rhythm.

Hey at least the DJ was good.

'What do you do?' asked Rachel.

'Temp.'

'Yeah Marla told us.'

'What do you want to be?' asked Rachel.

'Rich,' I replied

'You'll have to get him first.'

'No, *I* want to be rich.' I emphasised the pronoun and they laughed.

'Do you have a fellow, then?' asked Rachel.

'No, I don't.'

Sharon smiled. 'Marla told us you'd been dumped.'

Yeah and she told me you two were known locally as Sharon the Canyon and Rachel the Sword Swallower.

'Good riddance to bad rubbish hey,' and we raised our glasses.

All of them had fellas but Saturday was girls' night out.

'Don't get us wrong, we're not that sort.'

'What sort?'

'We don't mess around or nothing, just a bit of fun, a bit of a flirt.' They didn't have to justify themselves to me.

There was a main dance floor and we took to it, to limber up. Toowit Twoo Marla dirty danced around me, singing aloud as she strutted her stuff. Sharon and Rachel disappeared into the toilet emerging twenty minutes later, their faces touched up and their eyes dilated.

'What are you on?' I asked.

'Nothing,' they answered fearing I'd try and scab some off them, but whatever it was, it was crap 'cause after an hour they are both freaking out.

'Paid twelve quid for that.'

'Bloody outrage if you ask me.'

I was in need of an independent spirit, a sexually alert type who could tell by a glance I was desperate. Mission plausible: to find someone eager to fuck, who needed to fuck and have done with it, no remorse, no recriminations and no small talk, or as little as possible. My visual preceptors skirted the circuit. An Italian stallion with bulging trousers was eyeing Marla, pity that, he might have been fun. He was on his own, had circled us a couple of times, was dancing on our outskirts. He edged me out, weaved his way closer to Marla and I found myself in front of a gaggle of public school boys guffawing on the border of the dance floor. Not my type, too close knit, too clever by half, you'd not get one of their kind alone, not on a first date.

In the mirrored bar I caught my reflection, I was never good at tag.

'Three Bacardies and a tequila,' I shouted to the barman, squashed up at the front. Damnit I looked innocent, pseudo innocent, not like I fucked. I momentarily wished I'd borrowed something off Marla.

'Awight, avin' a good time,' screeched Marla and I thought I'd be deaf by the end of the evening. 'I'm just going to take a breather.'

She squeezed by me, the Italian trotting along beside her.

She had moved three paces northward and two paces east when I heard her squeal. Marla my mate was being savagely lynched by a yob. Six inches of heel had met with his foot and he was vocalising his annoyance in a most ungentlemanly manner.

'I'm sorry,' says Marla swishing her hair. 'Didn't see you there.' He wasn't impressed, did not feel pressed upon to let this incident slide.

'Hey, leave her,' demanded Luigi intervening with mucho macho gusto.

Yob's eyes did a semicircle, glanced an advancing bouncer, retreated. 'Cunt,' and he let her go.

I had caught a whiff, a faint sniff of trouble, I love that smell, it reeks of promise. It reeks of my type. He had aroused my interest, most intriguing, positively alluring. A bow-legged denim clad cowboy with the profile of a condensed Marlboro man. A definite 'fucker', perhaps a contender. A succulent yob in his prime and me knickers already agush. He pushed me aside to get to the bar, oblivious to my threat.

I suspected him being of indiscriminate taste, always got what he wanted, always in control but strictly dirty, either attracted to truly little girls or women. Big girls dressed as little girls wouldn't hold much interest. How to snare him without batting an eyelid. I'd have to spin a yarn and I set myself the challenge.

Rachel and Sharon were holding fort. Full of indignation I told them about Marla's fracas. Doing my best Iago, I pointed out the guys in question hoping to spurn them to take some action and initiate proceedings with said males yonder. Their ears pricked up, no one was going to diss their mate and they reckoned they could get their own back with a bit of 'state of the ear' teasing.

'Watch this,' said Rachel.

I did, I could learn a lot from Rachel. She walked straight over and accidentally bumped into one. She made out someone pushed her and it 'weren't 'er faul'.

Rachel was dressed in strips of tight Lycra wrapped at intervals around her body. The front of her dress was sodden and one of the guys offered to lick her dry. 'A drink will do,' she said and the bloke leant over the bar to order her one.

Round one to us.

'Cheers. If you're feeling lonesome me and me mates are over there.' She pointed to our table. Marla arrived back flushed. I noticed she was no longer wearing tights.

'Anyone want a dance?'

'Sure,' I say.

'Awight, enjoying yourself? Great innit,' she shouted, 'I love this place.'

It didn't take long before the opening gambit was acted upon. The corners of the puzzle setting up parameters. Surprise, surprise and who'd have believed it unless they had witnessed it with their own eyes, only what do you know, but didn't the lads wander over.

Except Yob that is, he was elsewhere.

Sharon and Rachel wiped smiles across their respective faces, repositioned their breasts and ruched up their skirts.

There was one each, Paul hooked on me, Peter on Rachel and John on Sharon. They had come to spread their message, discuss themes of a sinful nature and of loving thy neighbour. Paul had a cheeky grin, looked like an ape, wore a gold chain and gold flat-topped ring. Those mock royal stamps to seal letters or implant in people's heads. He was being evasive about what he did,

'A bit of this, bit of that, know what I mean?'

Sure I do, Doleman. I was getting agitated, Yob was not where he was supposed to be. I was worried it wasn't going to happen.

I was on the wrong turf, the wrong territory.

I was on my fourth or fifth tequila.

We forgot about Marla 'cause she had forgotten us. Her stallion was galloping her around the boogie woogie dance floor. Paul wedged himself in close beside me, casually let his arm rest behind my head. Apparently I was taken, sold to the man on my left. He fancied his chances and then the Chosen One reappeared. Yob stood facing me.

'Eh Gary awright,' says Paul, specifically referring to me.

Yob looked me over.

'Not bad,' came the reply.

Must have him now, fuelled by tequila confidence, had to get him in. I had no set plan and was trusting to fate. I sank further towards Paul, the intention being to evoke interest through lack of acknowledgement. I hoped I had read him right. Gary was leader of the gang, Jesus to his disciples. He held court over our table, entertained us with tales of nigger cunt bouncers giving him grief and then regretting it.

'Impressive,' said I contemptuously, throwing the killer look, the shuddering stare that takes years to master. Fuck it I had to say something to get his attention. He reacted appropriately, aimed to take me down a peg or two. The dice rolled and stakes were called and I raised class barriers so he could crash into me.

Then half an hour down the line and on my sixth or seventh tequila, Sharon and Rachel slouched off to the bog to determine if they were prick teasing or should actually go for it. In their absence Gary moved in on my other side. Whether he was playing around or pushing his luck, his hand was on my leg. Paul remained in his natural state, oblivious, and under the table Gary's hand was travelling northward about to hit my nub.

109

Well rub a nub nub, two men in a club maybe it was a set-up, maybe Paul was in on it too, a double helping, now, now, don't get greedy.

I crossed my legs and trapped him. I did so want to trap him.

Then . . .

shot through with tequila, I was greening at the gills, could almost smell the forthcoming puke.

'I really must be going.'

Taking my leave just as things were getting hot, getting sticky. Hot, sticky, viscous and bleary . . . OK I admit defeat, I'm saturated, stifled, seeing double really must be going, 'Really must be going.'

Jesus woman keep it together, breathe in, breathe out, in, out.

'Monday Marla.'

'Are you awright?'

'Tired, shattered, Monday.'

Sea legs carry me, exit out, lights slur vision, pushed past punters, collecting drips of sweat. I needed some air. Air repeating myself, regurgitating words and I swallowed just in time. I held my jacket loosely, dragged it across the road, skimming dirt from off the street. Slumped to a step to consolidate myself, let the cold race through me, head between my legs, not quite but lolling, breathe in, breathe out and soon I was feeling the cold. I lit a cigarette. Good God but you are good to me and I'm only messing when I say I don't believe in you.

'D'you have a light?'

Yobman, I knew it, just knew it, he'd followed me outside to make sure I was OK, ah sweet.

'Budge,' he demanded and sat down beside me on the

step, his hand back where it belonged. 'Marla sent me out. Are you all right?'

I was beginning to get a second wind and this time it was dry. I was feeling refocused. 'Awful, you wouldn't mind getting me cab would ya?'

'Walk you to the door if you want.'

And further.

He was quite good looking, in this light especially.

'So I got to you in the end,' I said.

'You think you're really special.'

'Yeah, well we were bound to have something in common.'

A little slap and tickle
    a bumpy ride back and . . .
'Home,' I slurred.

'Daddy's little rich girl,' he sneered eyeing up everything but me.

'Full of assumptions aren't you?' and I grabbed him by his denim lapels, pulling him close into me.

And then there I was legs akimbo like the skinflick girls only my arsehole wasn't airbrushed out, lying on my back thinking of forbidden patent shoes reflecting young girls' knickers and telephone directories placed on boys' knees, providing of course you ever got lucky enough to sit on one. Convent stories confirmed by Bea. I should have taken Bea up on her offer, gone out with her instead of Marla. Too late, too late.

He seemed to be enjoying himself and sure wasn't I having a wail of a time. The last thing a *cailín deas óg* thinks of is England, that really would be shameful.

So it's lie back girl, lie back . . . and hope the room stops spinning.

Bruises

Candle flames flickered either side of a wide iron bed, a warm glow of tenderness casting shadows. She lay on her front, slumbering, naked. His hand gently gliding up and down her back. From the base of her spine to her neck and beyond. Under her hair exploring. Creeping fingers towards her face and brushing back fine strands hiding fine features. Her hair tossed aimlessly barring him from her. Brushing it back, he stroked her cheek, ran a fingertip over a red lip.

'Sweet one' wistfully whispered gazing down upon her, ever so tempting, he could gaze for hours.

A return journey and his hand moved back down the length of her spine and rested a moment. His hand laid flat, the width of her, star-shaped fingers touching either waist side, tiny, a glimmer in his eye. A speck of clog dust and he blink blinkered and rubbed red eyesore. Eyes sore from gazing. Her skin smooth as calf suede, baby soft and he glimpsed small hairs, a chickenpox scar, a beauty mark, a bruise. Purple bluish mark. Sensitive skin, sensual. Barely perceptible but bruised. He was always so gentle with her. Baffled. Spotted another lower down. Yellow dirty brown, skin marred. Maybe? Could be the light.

He leant down lower, to take a closer look. Bearing down upon her, prodding her right there, would mark her reaction. She winced, waved, raised a hand to swat him away.

'Am I tickling you?'

'Mmmmmm.'

She rolled on to her side curling up and away from him.

She had been waiting for him when he arrived. As requested.

It was not too much to ask that she be there for him, he demanded nothing from her, just that she be there for him. Gentle with his pleas, a most gentle manner. Tender with his touches, tendered skin.

The lights were on, the car pulled up outside the mews, the besuited suitor relieved to be back. The country air had got to him, one can have too much of this rural idyll. In no time at all, no motorway hold-up, double quick they could spend the whole evening together. Softly, softly he would surprise her, key in the lock, left luggage under the stairs.

She had been lying on the divan, stretched out, eyes closed to music playing loudly. Haunting sounds, melodies to escape to, entrancing. He slithered up on her from behind, quietly his arms laden with gift boxes, ribbon wrapped and tempting.

Enchanted and he started to hum softly, to gently penetrate her space. He didn't want to shock her, twitch, tense, shush, and he bent over his sleeping beauty. To wake her with a kiss. She flick-opened her eyes had imagined a prince.

'Did I frighten you?'

'No, no.'

A king bearing gifts for his little goddess, her eyes lit up when she saw him. Ahhh, hush, kiss first, ahhhhh, second kiss.

Like a child at Christmas, eager to see what he had bought her. Impatient to discover the delights in store. Patience, patience, all in good time, he wanted to see her. Naked, he needed to get out of his weary travelled suit and wash away the residue of wife association.

They shared a shower. Children playing in puddles wet through, haphazardly splashing, soaped up, creaming, hot jet, splutter, splatter and childlike she pulled at him.

'Now can I open my presents, Marcus?'

He told her she could open one.

'Only one?' she sighed, spirit dampened, towel dried and powder pampered. Stood behind her in the looking-glass, Marcus reflected on the pleasing image.

Disrobed. He let her open one box. Hoped she would wear the dress inside it. He bought it specially, already a picture in his mind. Coloured tissue paper, silk soft, skin tight, cut low. She looked so pretty in it, pretty as a picture, a perfect fit.

They went out to eat. Marcus was hungry and the fridge was bare, the fridge was always bare. He decided he would like to try out a new restaurant, it had just opened, the reviewers' views dribbling off the page.

He reserved a table keeping an eye on her as she applied her make-up, dabbed perfume behind her earlobes, then she twirled in front of him when she was ready. He liked to show her off, was proud to have her by his side. His arm cast over her shoulder, shielding her from strangers' stares.

Stranger and stranger. Onlookers looking on, whispers at the stir they caused.

They sat at a round table, a smiling waitress brought over the menu and small basket of bread. She was tempted to nibble, her hand reaching forward in the attempt to do so, but Marcus said it would ruin her appetite.

Then the waitress returned, ready to take their orders.

She said, 'I'd like the fish.'

'No, no the lamb would be better.' Marcus suggested the lamb, it would complement the chosen wine. 'We shall have the lamb pink.'

The waitress commended his choice, departed and Marcus relaxed back into his chair to tell her of the things he had been doing.

Marcus was on one of his stopovers. Back in London for the next few days before being claimed by family or business.

'Dreadful business.' He told her a friend of the family was in trouble. 'Stupid boy got himself into a terrible mess, can't understand it at all.'

She agreed, she hadn't understood either.

Of course Marcus would do everything in his power to help sort things out; if he could be of any assistance he would.

She agreed. She said if there was anything she could do herself, she would.

And Marcus laughed. 'Ah sweet one.'

The best of her intentions dismissed, there was really nothing she could do, Marcus had it all under control. Marcus had checked out the solicitor and apparently he was good. But she had stopped listening, ceased eating. He noticed.

'Don't you like your food?' he asked and she said it was fine but she didn't feel so hungry. She laughed it off.

'If I have any more, Marcus I'll burst out of this dress.'

He continued with his story, was mimicking Gilly: 'It's just one thing after another, Marcus, why would he do a thing like that . . . such a handsome young man, he could get any woman, anyone. It just doesn't make sense.'

Marcus had assured Gilly it wasn't so bad. From what he understood, the case was fairly cut and dried, the likelihood of Richard being sentenced was minimal. Marcus was going to see Richard the next day, see if he could be of any further assistance.

'I told Gilly she really mustn't take these things to heart.' Marcus raised his eyes. 'She tends to veer on the side of hysteria.'

But she really wasn't listening.

Marcus declared the lamb delicious. He took a piece of bread from the basket to soak the blood from the plate.

Arms linked they homeward strolled, sighing contentment of flavoursome breath to foghorn their journey. And back in the present, present time.

He had bought her a leatherbound book. A bound book of sonnets with gilt edges and gilt lettering. He'd written her a note. A personal note to express his feelings and he marked a sonnet which he thought befitting.

'You're a good man, Marcus,' she grinned up at him.

'Am I?'

'Of course, you're very good at being a man.'

He bought her a silver frame, just like the one on the

sideboard, a matching pair. She could put a picture of them inside. How fitting a picture of the pair of them, side by side. He really shouldn't have but he couldn't help himself and he'd bought her a camera.

She threw her arms around him, hugged him, excited as a puppy, couldn't wait to take some pictures, patience, patience, there was a roll of film included, maybe later.

'The frame, it's missing . . .'

'What?' She wasn't listening. Absorbed by the complicated camera, in that high tech way, few buttons and millions of functions.

'The silver frame on the sideboard by the candle . . .'

'What?'

'The silver frame, the crystal candlesticks.' Double negative.

She looked around at him, to the sideboard, bereft of articles, her heart sank, Christ.

'Oh Marcus, I'm sorry, I meant to tell you, was going to tell you . . . I' – She jumped to her feet dragged him back to the divan. 'Say you'll forgive me.'

She sat astride him.

'You'll think this really silly, promise not to laugh.'

He looked at her and she cupped her hands around his face.

'Marcus I'm so sorry I . . . I . . . broke them,' And she scrunched up her face waiting for a forthcoming explosion.

'How?'

She said she had been dancing,

Alone?

like you do, as a kid, in front of the mirror . . .

got carried away and knocked them over, sorry, sorry,

sorry, say you'll forgive me and she kissed, kissed, kissed, him.

'What were you listening to?'

'Emerson Lake & Palmer.'

'Show me how you danced.'

'Might, might not . . .'

'Go on.'

'Well put some music on.'

They moved from off the divan.

'OK but not here, I'll dance but only if you show me how to work this camera.' And she led him into the master bedroom.

It had to be . . . could only be, Yobman and his sticky fingers. Glass shattered but silver cracked is an impossibility. She hadn't noticed. Christ, and she hoped nothing else was missing, distract him, distract him, dance for him, dance for him, his eyes were burning up, enveil him, seven times to weave about him, cast a spell of utter distraction and seductively she moved, moved sensually, slowly, hypnotic.

Love made and Marcus had been looking at her, thinking.

Two bruises though he couldn't be sure of the ownership, double-cross, it had crossed his mind. A pair of candlesticks and a silver frame. Framed. Stranger and stranger. Candles flickered by a big iron bed casting aspersions on love's honour.

Still, Marcus bent across her to blow out the flame, then rolled back to his side to snuff out the other.

Bea's predictions

It was driving her insane, round the bend, back again. All calm on the Berian front and it had Bea worried. Basically if Bea didn't have anything to worry about she'd go to pieces. The more worries she had the more alive and in control she felt. In effect worry was a good thing although it didn't solve her problems. The problem being Brian was ideal but was she his ideal and how could she be sure?

For sure, for sure, Brian had been acting the exemplary boyfriend since her birthday. Something was up.

Her birthday.

Another year closer to her ultimate deadline, another line inching into her forehead. Twenty-seven years to be accounted for, each one heavy weighing like a milestone round her neck. She thought Brian had forgotten, had heard the plop of post on Ruth's natural fibre mat and whilst hardly resounding, down those stairs Bea ran. A mere two cards to acknowledge her existence and a bill. The first, from her folks, containing 200 punts and the second from Gatsby, the family hound. Her mother hadn't even bothered to dip his paw in ink, she just wrote 'Woof Gatsby'.

There was a homemade card and a secondhand book entitled *Karma in Crisis* from Ruth, and at work a bunch of flowers from Ian, which though nice, were not such a surprise as Bea had ordered them the night before, gift buying coming under her span of responsibilities. It's the thought that counts and Brian's were conspicuously lacking. The least she had expected was a card. She called Brian up to give him a mouthful, mounted her high horse and refused to get off. Didn't know what hit him and before Brian could get a word in edgeways, a small parcel appeared and was placed on Bea's desk. Beautifully wrapped and ribboned and beneath the paper was a rectangular black box, looking a bit like a jewellery box, though too big for a ring and inside was the most gorgeous, thoughtful, amazingly amazing present she had ever received.

A watch, and lifting it from its case to examine it she discovered the following engraved on the underside, BECAUSE TIME WITH YOU FLIES. She started to cry, pressed redial and told Brian she was the luckiest girl in the universe and didn't deserve someone like him and he agreed and told her to be ready at eight because he had booked a table in a restaurant so cool he had had to pull in five favours just so they could go. He told her the watch was water resistant and she said that was brilliant, she would wait till later for him to wrap it round her wrist and promised never to take it off.

She held it to her ear, to listen to its ticking, forgetting digitals didn't.

And from that moment not a bad word had passed between them and Bea feared in case this phase was transient, that underneath their seemingly perfect veneer a cyst like substance lurked.

Happiness was unnerving.

If only life was a simple and straightforward journey to the other side. She had been reading *Karma in Crisis*, there was no other side, it was all circles, never-ending swings and roundabouts. She'd been taking deep breaths, then exhaling air in bursts of I love Brian, I am at one with Brian, I accept Brian as he is. A need was gnawing away at her, her instincts obscured by neurosis. If only she could find a more objective analysis of their relationship. She looked around for a suitable third party, an onlooker who could tell if she was on the right track and who was not her mother. A person of great perceptivity able to foretell the future and put her mind at rest.

Bea was not a superstitious person, to be honest she was rather contemptuous of the supernatural, mysticism being double Dutch to herself but on this occasion, the signs could not be ignored.

Then one night curled up in her jim-jams (nightdresses had a habit of creeping up her back with the intent to strangle and she would wake up choking, her head shrouded in nylon), Bea, drowsing off, was half listening to a late night love train session on the radio. Sweet talking syrup soothing Samson was focusing in on love, how to find it, how to keep it, how to know it's real and with him in the studio was Soraya, rrr, grrrrr, spiritual love healer, 'Yooow Soraya, thanks for taking time out to be with us. We'll be talking in a couple of minutes but first an old favourite of mine and a definite favourite of yours, 10cc with "Zoom".'

Soraya's voice softly permeated Bea's slumbered thought waves with words of love and the offer of a guiding hand to those needing to know the truth. Next morning humming 'just one look and then my heart went Boom', Bea was on the tube reading the classifieds over someone's shoulder when her beady eye noticed the headline BE AWARE: Soraya, Spiritualist to the Rich and Famous, from a long line of Eastern Sorcerers, had a special offer on. A full hour for the price of a half-session, automatic trance on demand, as seen on TV, High Profile Clients, accuracy vouched for, tarot with clairvoyance plus and this was what hooked Bea, it was the woman from the radio show.

That same evening Bea's mind fairly spasmed when she got the weirdest wrong number. Some guy rang up and asked for Soraya.

Pardon? Soraya? No there was no one by that name in the flat, what number was he looking for? Ehh yeah, this is the number but no, no, there was definitely not anyone by that name here, yes, she was sure, where had he got the number from? A classified. Something strange was going on, this was no coincidence, could she talk dirty anyhow? No, she couldn't.

Bea booked a session. A morning off work for woman's trouble and found herself walking down a back alley, discovered herself in front of a dilapidated building, air thick with dust, the kind of place Norman Bates would call home. Mounting rickety stairs, she could hear the wind whistle, the creak of the steps, the distant drip of a tap. Her bag clutched tight to her chest, her heart thump thumping, wanting her mammy, oh God. This by God was too, too spooky by far.

A small woman with crinkly skin in a very bad wig greeted her at the top of the stairs. She was wearing a soup-stained pink polyester polo neck, a black crêpe skirt the hemline hanging and fluffy slippers.

'Bea, I presume. Welcome, come in, come in. I am with a client but take a seat in the parlour and I'll be with you in a jiffy.' She took Bea's hands, covered them with both of hers. 'Warm hands, bite your nails?'

'No they just don't grow.'

'Ohh . . . I sense you are a little tense, you're safe with me though, only good tidings here, only good things. Relax, relax, nothing terrible is going to happen.'

She showed Bea into a tiny reception area, a threadbare sofa, crystals and candles galore. On the wall hung autographed pictures of so-called famous clients, none of whom Bea recognised.

Sitting thumb twiddling, Bea listened to Soraya's singsong voice from the other room. Eventually the door in the far corner creaked open and Soraya reappeared, alone.

'A client from the other side, sorry to have kept you waiting.'

The inner room was dark, the window blackened, a small circular table with a crystal ball, decks of cards and a clutter of chairs, the atmosphere incense heavy with thick velvet brocade hanging off the walls. It stank of cats' pee and Bea counted six cats lounging on cushions fat, immobile and stuffed.

Freakier and freakier and what the hell had she let herself in for. What in the name of God was she doing there anyhow? Bea thought about backing out, making excuses but Soraya closed the door behind her. Bea thought she heard a click. Soraya was babbling about first times; yeah said Bea, when I was seventeen.

'Really? really? I was married at ten to a sea merchant it didn't last very long, back in those days if you were gifted

124

they had you killed, a knife to the jugular, one foul swipe, it was awful, dreadful. He wasn't the sensitive sort.'

Bea paled.

'My first life, oh I've had many marriages, many first times. Some hellish, others less hellish, I still keep in touch with my ninth husband, you know. He was wonderful, a right charmer, what he didn't know about snakes . . . swallowed alive, alive, took three days to digest but I'm babbling, babbling . . . well now what can I do for you, the cards or your palm?'

'Mmmm, the cards . . . no my palm . . . mmm . . . OK my cards.'

'Now I want you to relax, take a deep breath and shuffle the deck.'

Bea's lungs expanded, then exhaled with 'I am one Brian, Brian loves me how he is.' It was all very unsettling, to be sat facing a strange woman who knew more about you than you did yourself, who held your future in her hands.

Soraya warned Bea to withhold questions till the end cause if she stopped midstream she would lose concentration. She popped a tape into the recorder which much to Bea's relief, meant she wouldn't have to take shorthand, and began.

'Well you're in a bit of a conundrum, I see?'

'I am, am I?'

'Yes, hmmmm, interesting, you have a boyfriend.'

'Brian,' Bea blurted. She bit her lip had heard it said it was better to keep quiet, not give too much away.

'You are very much in love with him.'

'Mmmm.'

'But you are entering a new phase in your life.'

'The dry patch?' Bea ventured ever hopeful.

'Perhaps but he's not the only man, there is another one,

in the shadows and he thinks about you often and he loves you.'

'That can't be right, are you sure?'

'There are two men, definitely, one dark, the other fair.'

'Are you sure?'

'The cards don't lie. Look, the fair one faces away but is looking back at you with longing.'

Soraya pushed forward a dandy Jack of Diamonds.

Bea was perplexed, there was no way it was Donald, he had dark brown hair. 'Shay it must be Shay.'

'No it's not Shay . . . he's across the water living in a closet.'

Bea's mouth gaped.

'See, the cards are correct, I told you so, Soraya sees all. Not so many questions please. You have control, both men desire you. You will come to a crossroads and be forced to make a decision.'

'What decision?'

'That is your choice.'

'But what if I make the wrong one?'

'You will face the consequences.'

Chrissakes Bea had wanted clarity, her worries doubled now, double the choice, double the trouble. Who the hell was this fair man? The dark one had to be Brian and the fair one, who? who? It wasn't fair.

'What about marriage?'

'Yes.'

'When?'

'When you have made up your mind. Look darlin' I'm losing concentration on the love front, let's move on to something else, time's pressing.'

Ian. It could be Ian her boss, he wasn't exactly fair: highlights, Essex boy highlights. Please God it is not Ian, anyone but him.

'Excuse me Soraya but can't you give me an initial or something for the fair guy?'

Soraya motioned Bea to shut up.

'There is another woman. A woman who the dark one adores.'

What other woman? Brian and another woman, no, no, now Bea really couldn't bear it.

'She is on your side and is not a threat.'

A woman who was not a threat, sure anyone female to come within ten foot of Brian was a potential hazard.

'This woman will be a help to you in your goals, though you may not realise it. Oh this is good.'

'What? what?'

'Big change in store on the work front, within a year you will be in another position.'

Bea didn't want another job, she was happy where she was, must mean the sack, two men, a woman and the sack. Great, this was going great.

'You mustn't fret. Work will come easily and you will prosper. I see a position of power in a small company by a canal.'

Soraya told Bea to concentrate more on herself and not to worry, it would all come out in the wash, the proof she said would be in the pudding, purple was a good colour and she would win money this week. Her father would have an operation on his doodah before the year was out, she could see a moving terrace and squashed dog.

'What do you mean a squashed dog?'

'A woman, blood on her hands and dog on a tyre.'

The card, Christ the card from Gatsby, she knew something was amiss, hadn't the card been signed by her mother . . .

'More immediately a long-distance call and tears.'

Her mother, she would have to ring her mother the minute she got out of here.

'Well that's that. Lots of change, good cards, you're a lucky woman.'

Lucky, lucky – had the woman heard herself talk, which bit exactly was lucky?

'Now remember nothing is written in stone and things may change or be reinterpreted, that'll be forty pounds, cash, cheque or credit card, the tape will be an extra twenty.'

'I thought the tape was included?'

'No, it's an extra, everyone's entitled to little extras these days.'

Bea counted out forty. Forget the tape, forget it all, she ran to the nearest call box and accused her mother of murder.

'I didn't want to go upsetting you, Bea. Sure he was very old, and having only the three legs, he didn't have a chance.'

Bea had grown up with Gatsby, they were more than dog and mistress. They were good friends.

'Upsetting me? upsetting me?' Her knees crumpled beneath her and she sank to the piss-stained concrete of the phone booth, howling. A scratch card lay by her feet, a thousand smackeroonies for the taking. She didn't notice; doubled over with anguish she tore it to pieces. Her mother as distraught as herself and they weren't the only ones, some fella was down on his hands and knees scouring the pavement, cursing till kingdom come.

What a life, eh? Some days there just ain't no point in stirring. Bea would stick to her own religion in future, it really doesn't do to be messing around with the occult, far safer not knowing what's what. Her prospects bleak, her dog dead, Brian about to have an affair, Ian secretly fantasising over her. It was all too much, she called work to say she was taking the rest of the day off, hurried home and held her own private Gatsby memorial.

Ugly fat girl

Ugly fat girl, ugly fat girl, there ain't no fun for ugly fat girl.

How many come-ons does ugly fat girl get?

How many compliments? roses? favours? sweeteners? wolf whistles?

None.

No opening doors, no help when weighed down with bags, no free drinks, meals or anything. She may run for the bus but she'll still miss it. She can smile all she likes, flutter her eyes, but no one will notice, there will be no response.

The only attention ugly fat girl gets is when schoolboys bark at her.

She is routinely refused from clubs, doormen look her up and down, we're full up, Missy, members only, private party. She has never had a bed partner who wasn't completely pissed blind. She has received three Valentine cards in her lifetime, all self-sent.

There are absolutely no perks of femininity for ugly fat girl.

She could be the cleverest woman in the world, the wittiest, most charming, astonishingly, fantastically, Nice Person, which she is but at the end of the day, no matter how hard she tries, she will always be ugly fat girl.

Ugly fat girl is kind and thoughtful and gives up her free

time to work for charities, towards the betterment of mankind, she is always giving, giving, giving. She believes in the furtherance of civilisation, joins radical groups with similar-looking people, fights for causes, for the less advantaged, for endangered mammals, and writes regularly to prisoners. She wants the world to be a better place, for everyone to get along.

She wants, she wants . . .

She has phone sex, rings up chat lines, hello, hello, and describes herself as a long-legged beauty, she puts on a sexy voice and coos, *Hi there handsome*, she calls herself Soraya, she stretches out the name, *Sooraaayaaa*, her phone bill is enormous. The best party she ever went to was a masked ball.

Ugly fat girl may trip in the street or be mugged or attacked, she may have received a big black eye in the very centre of one of the biggest cities in the world and not one person would stop and ask her if she is OK. Not one person . . . and penniless she could have got on the tube sure once she explained the situation they would let her away with it. But no they would fine her ten quid. She would be fined a tenner for flouting regulations.

Ugly fat girl dreams of passion. She has a fantasy. She thinks about standing alone on a stage, on a podium in a huge spotlight. Imagines she is the sexiest person alive and looks beautiful, her hair done by a famous hairdresser and her make-up applied by a Hollywood make-up artist. The stage is strewn with flowers, red roses piling up by the dozen and boxes of chocolates with fresh cream centres. The auditorium is packed to overflowing, hundreds and thousands of males stand before her, howling cries of adulation. She cannot hear herself think, her ears are bombarded by an infinite array of adoring descriptions. She is blinded by flashing cameras, zoom lenses and all she has to do is stand still and smile. She doesn't have to move, she doesn't have to say a thing. As she rubs her hands over her famous waistline the crowd goes wild, the crowd is hysterical, and by the time her hands reach her voluptuous breasts, the crowd has been whipped into a frenzy and they run towards the stage, there is no stopping them, they topple over one another to get to her first, to have a chance of touching her, to be near her, feel her breath upon their tongues, in the rush some are trampled under foot, others overcome by emotion, ecstatic, euphoric even catatonic and she is carried off on a wave of love, she floats on a sea of hands passing from one pair to another, to another, to the chanting cries of Sorayyaaa . . . Soraayyaa.

Ruth picked up the receiver, her digits on the pulse . . . hello . . . hello . . .

The Pickup

'Good afternoon, Anal and Renal.'

Anal and bloody Renal, I ask you and I'm still at it. How is it possible, I must have slipped into someone else's destiny. Of course I blame Margaret, thought we had it all in the palm of our hands and then recession slaps us in the face at our graduation ceremony. Four years of the life of Riley, of cobblestones and acres of books and then ... And then, congratulations and a piece of paper with Latin scrawled all over it points the way to the nearest dole office. What do you mean I have to get a job, what do you mean I have to make a living, aha winked the bank manager, 'What have you been studying for all these years?'

'Knowledge good sir, KNOWLEDGE.'

'And what's it good for?' he quips with a glint in his eye.

I mustered a response.

'Making sure reality stays at arm's length. Constructing ivory towers to imprison myself in, sir.' Click of my heels, slap of my forehead with a smarmy salute and then he helped me close my account. The bank manager walked me to the door, his hand on my shoulder.

'Did you never hear of the Milk Round?'

I was never partial to milk, always favoured the stronger stuff, always to be found down the buttery discussing work rather than doing it, or on occasion having a go at the yard of ale with Bea on the steps of the GMB. I tended to splutter but Bea showed a natural aptitude for it and entered all yard of ale contests, won a few competitions, which was quite an achievement seeing as she was pitched against rugger men. She reached her height of fame with a front-page picture in the *Irish Times* during rag week, but her mother threw a fit and banned her from drinking beer,

'Think of your waistline darling,' and she increased Bea's allowance so she could afford shorts.

Work, such a dirty word and I slowly realised I would have to do some. I started scanning the papers' vacancies and quickly realised you had to have experience. So I packed my bags and went in search of some.

It was precisely 5 hours 19 minutes and 57, see I'd been counting the seconds.

Brring, Brrring . . .

'Good afternoon, Anal and Renal.'

'Of course it's Anal and Renal, dipstick,' an internal call, an over-confident upper English class accent was haw haw hawing and I was on the receiving end. Stupid girl, he's thinking. The Irish accent didn't help.

I had the right to remain silent.

'Get out the wrong side of bed this morning, what?'

'Whatever side of the bed I get out of is my business shithead, do you understand?'

The phone went dead.

He he he . . .

He rang the supervisor:

'Does that young woman want to keep her job?'

No, no she doesn't. Go fuck yourselves I say giving them the finger and the switchboard was hopping.

'Temp to Temp Controller, come in Temp Controller.'

'Vice versa, copy.'

'Cretinous crap, refuse to take, bailed out but still alive, copy.'

'Not to worry, call in on Monday, copy.'

'Will do, over and out.'

Repercussions are minimal for a here today gone tomorrow sort of person. So next week I will have something new to look forward to. A spanking new job with spanking new people or spankers as I call them. And so it goes on. I left Marla a couple of months back, promising to call. It was a laugh working with her. It must be said over the years I have learned a lot, I can file my nails as good as any manicurist.

I faxed my time sheet and enough. Ta-ra and bumpsadaisy to Anal and Renal. If I had stayed any longer, I think I would have had a hernia.

I have had enough.

Some day soon I'll step back and let the state take care of me. Sign my name on the dotted line and take it easy like the little bunny in the chocolate ad. A change is as good as a rest and I needed a bit of both.

'What's a girl like you doing in a place like this?'

'Hustling.'

Funny us meeting like that.

We'd been on the whiskies. A fine drink, such a comfort to the liver. An overwhelming desire to get paralytic had fallen upon me. My system needed a thorough cleansing, so I went in search of a pub, a place worthy of the name, with real alcoholics. Turned out it wasn't such a hard challenge.

Sat down the back I was doing a crossword, watching the herd work their wages. The place was packed till seven, then emptied as quick as a Sassenach spirit measure and the commuters commuted to their pastures green.

'Come home with me,' he pleaded. 'I need to feel human.'

He had plonked himself down on the stool opposite doing a crossword of his own. We remained silent till he leant forward and said,

'Clue, woman running round fore part of doomed ship is hard to identify.'

'Do you mind?'

His suit was dark, well cut, definitely designer, shirt crisp white with the top button undone. I'm such a sucker for suits. As I bent down to retrieve a pack of cigarettes from out of my bag, I snuck a look at his shoes, plain black sturdy leather lace-ups, his knees touching the table top. He told me his father had made him do crosswords from the age of six to increase his vocabulary.

'Have you cracked it?' he asked

'Yeah, ages ago,' I lied. I had become bored, filled the empty boxes with any old letters. He looked impressed. He looked impressive.

'Would you like a drink?'

Two strangers easing into conversing mode. And after three drinks we were having a nice time. His eyes were blue and nose large; clean shaven, pale, smooth skinned with a scar running vertically along his left eye, hair plentiful and a warming smile.

'I've had such a tiresome day.' Nice voice, slow talker, words unrushed falling from lips dry.

'Likewise Mister if it's going to be tiresome I don't want to know.' I smiled and it hurt, my lips stretched that bit too much and I could feel the muscles straining upward.

He asked me what I did.

'Pass,' I answered.

He told me he was a solicitor and I said, 'Strange I was with one only yesterday'.

The whiskies kindled a conversation and led to a spark which led to a flame. He told me stories and told them well; engrossed for a while I forgot where I was.

And three drinks further on we were spewing our hatred of all and sundry. All those missed opportunities, mistakes, let-downs.

He told me I should travel, I told him I had.

He said the world is a big place. I agreed.

I was warm and loose, my tongue wagging. I could have told him a million things, a billion secrets, divulged all, for it would have been the drink talking. Maybe I did. Maybe stack loads of stuff fell out before I could swallow it back.

In the lucid world of drunkenness I was feeling myself, for it takes a fuzzy head to get things into perspective.

Soon enough the lights flickered and we got another round in.

'Come home with me,' he said.

I said nothing.

'Say yes.'

'You'd be putting words in my mouth, Mister.'

'Nod then.'

He informed me in all sincerity he hadn't been curled around a body for an age.

Strange, I never usually let men choose me, maybe he didn't, maybe 'it' just happened. I had to size him up, use my better judgement.

'Sidle up to sleep,' matter-of-factly spoken and he seemed like a nice man.

I wanted to say yes, to curl about you too.

I trusted my instincts and left.

It was a cold starry night, no cloud cover. Unusual for London the twinklers were out in full force and together we hurled a wish upwards may a cab come quick. Alcohol-diluted body heat being more a mental warmer and we were freezing. He wrapped me inside his coat and I felt his warmth on the corner of a pavement, waiting.

'You don't mind do you?'

'No, free will and all that.'

'I'd understand, if you got cold feet.'

'I do, I always have cold feet, I place a hot water bottle at the bottom of the bed.'

Nerves made me chatter stupidly. I hoped I read him right.

The talk ceased and we travelled silently, looking out opposite windows. He lived not too far from the city centre in a converted Victorian terrace, his flat on the top floor. We climbed the stairs and our breaths quickened, shortened, the impersonal encounter about to breach contract, we would become aware of ourselves.

'Nice,' I said before he had switched on the light.

'Nice,' I echoed when he switched it on.

My tongue had dried up and he poured me a large whiskey, my chest whistling from having smoked too much. And who would have thought it could have ended like this. His living room was large and airy, a massive sofa, prints on the wall, cluttered shelves with books, photos, small sculptures, plenty of technology, a computerised corner, fax, phones, the world at his fingertips and he's lonely.

I blurted it out, I had to, for his own safety of course. Spelt it out in black and white so there would be no chance of miscommunication, of repercussions.

No fucking.

'No,' he assured me. 'Let's pretend we are innocents.'

'Yeah I'm good at pretending,' I answered.

Split level, the bedroom upstairs and his comfortable bed smelt clean. My head was splitting, I was pulling myself from sleep to consciousness, a tiny moment when you can see time pass. Seconds perhaps before the evening fell into place and I realised where I was. Ah, frightening morning light so much safer in the darkness, blind drunk last night, lorded it a little, overstepped the mark.

His arms wrapped around me and his breath upon my neck. Warm, his body was warm, his sleepy arm heavy, freckled, mottled marble, I twisted inside his clasp to face his chest to implant soft kiss marks. He stirred and turned, freeing me. Quietly I rose and dressed. His place looked different in the morning light, stranger. Before I had just seen outlines, now I glimpsed a life. A photo of a child by his side. Brown curly hair. The same child, growing at intervals around the room. Didn't bother leaving a number.

I took a bus westward, the 28, only a couple of years older than myself. Bus sat, watching numbers get on and off, ceaseless people partaking in that Great British national pastime, queuing. I played spot the freak, saddo, nervous breakdown, loser, but the sun heavy shining made the windows reflective.

Then this little piggy went to market. Portobello to purchase nourishments. A promise made to keep the fridge stacked just in case an expectant visitor should arrive on the doorstep and surprise me. Definitely better not knowing what lies ahead. My new mobile phone lay trashed in its leather holder prematurely dead, cancer of the airwaves. I had plunged it into a banter bucket, well how was I to know it wasn't waterproof. See I keep getting these phone calls, filthy descriptions from a dirty old man. Not a nice thing to hear when you're taking a shower trying to wash the daily rind from off of your skin.

Saturday afternoon spent in the pastry shop, strong black coffee and the weekend papers. I guess I need some sugar to sweeten up my life and damn it Mister but you put me in a bad mood, made me feel. Christ he even made me laugh.

Off kilter and I really shouldn't let my mind wander. Let's face it, I am in a certain situation and as Bea would put it, you make your bed and you lie in it. Up to my neck in it. I'd like to change the covers, they are old and smothering. They smother me so that I cannot breathe. They weigh down heavy and I am lost beneath them. Yes I really must do something and I remind myself to leave a note out for the cleaning lady.

Damn damn damn I really have to get back on track.

Plan B

'Let me try and get this straight,' said Bea. 'You slept with a complete stranger.'

Lust had surely smacked Ian in the face for one morning he arrived at the office sporting a black eye and five very large and very painful hickies.

'How was I to know she was off her trolley?'

'Well firstly she actually slept with you, Ian.'

Bea dabbed Ian's neck with her cover-up cream in an effort to hide the offending marks.

'You should see my back. It's in shreds.'

'I can't believe you were so stupid, Ian. You slept with someone you don't know, had met that very night, Christ she could have been anyone, ughh the thought, it disgusts me.'

'I suppose you made Brian wait?'

'Eh . . . well that was different.'

On the sly Ian was a bit of a romantic, a big-nosed schmoozer on the blank page. He'd been replying to Lonely Hearts, bagging the odd shag now and again. It was a laugh till his sides started to hurt. There's S&M and then there's assault. His chest was battered, his back slashed. There was no denying it but a certain Sandra Hemming relished her pound of flesh, especially when it was Ian's she was pounding.

He arranged to meet her in a café bar: her photo had been passable but it was the tone of her letter that had him smitten.

Dear Tarzan,

Simply couldn't resist replying, you sound absolutely wild I'm fairly wild myself, a total tigress and I'd love to get my claws on you. I'm five foot one, brunette and gagging for it.

Lust

Sandra Hemming, xxxx (as in x-rated)

p.s. 10 inches . . . I hope you're not bragging!!!!
p.p.s. Call me now.

Bea was stunned, 'You met her, drank coffee and then . . .'

'Bea we skipped the coffee, she said it wasn't her cup of tea. I tell you this woman was forward, she didn't bother to shake my hand – went straight for the crotch.'

'No way.'

'I can't help it if women find me irresistible.'

'No way.'

'God's honest truth. She says to me, I've seen you, I like you, I want you, your place or mine?'

'So like, Ian, you just went along for the ride?'

'Of course.'

'Then what?'

'I take her to a hotel and we're on the job . . .'

'Good Christ,' groaned Bea.

'And this woman is wild, telling me to do this, that and the other.'

'Not the other!!' she squealed.

Sandra Hemming rang Ian every hour on the hour for the next two days from a call box on the corner of the street, stalking him between times plus maintaining a steady flow of oral obscenities.

Ian was not a happy man.

'Bea, I want her off my back.'

'Mmm . . . tricky.'

'What if you pretend you're my wife.'

'Don't be ridiculous Ian, a woman like that wouldn't be put off by a wife, you need a man.'

'What are you suggesting?'

'Get one of your male friends to throw a queeny wobbler.'

'Not on your life.'

'Don't be so stupid, if you can't stand her, what do you care if she thinks you're of the other persuasion?'

'I am not.'

'Ian, I know you're not.'

'It's disgusting.'

'Calm down, I was only suggesting you get one of your mates . . .'

'My mates . . . brilliant, Bea, so obvious, you're fantastic.'

'Oh thanks, Ian.'

'My mates –' he was already on the phone. 'I'll pass her off on one of them.'

Ian decided to quit the columns and move on to more stable stuff. Dating agencies offering Eastern babes for the price of a passport. He paid a whack of money, under guarantee of finding the perfect partner with a full refund in the event of dissatisfaction. Helping Ian complete one such form Bea reached a question on what one looks for in an ideal companion. Ian replied someone who didn't answer back.

'Seriously Ian, the ideal lifetime partner, who would you choose?'

'Someone to satisfy my cock, stomach and mounting laundry.'

'No seriously Ian.'

'I *am* being serious.'

Bea wrote a young attractive woman traditional at heart.

'If you ever want to get hitched Bea, get those three simple things right and I swear it will work.'

'Yeah like it's that easy.'

Ian's wise words set Bea thinking . . . Nah . . . no way . . . not possible, naaah . . . then again . . . naaaaaaah . . . well hold on now, it had been over six months, the m-word had yet to be mentioned, there hadn't been a whiff of it.

'A young attractive woman traditional at heart', it had a familiar ring to it. Bea's own aspirations weren't so far removed. So she had gone to college, graduated with a high II.1, was amongst the top of her year group but the fact remained, her mother chagrined, Bea had failed to secure some rich farmer's son. Her tutor suggested she study further but Bea declined the offer. The wormy world of academia didn't appeal nor had she been particularly career orientated. The idea of working her guts off for some international corporation ensuring a ridiculous salary, a pension fund to beat the blues and worldwide first-class travel was never a concrete picture. Ladders symbolised bad luck and Bea had no ambition to climb the corporate one; besides, heights weren't her forte although she wouldn't mind standing at the base and holding it steady. Provided it was the right ladder of course. Plagued by the back seat syndrome, Bea retained the belief that a girl could be a bit too clever for her own good. And yet at the same time it astounded Bea how Ian, a person of such low intelligence, could get a decent job and be considered good at it.

Yeah perhaps Ian was right, perhaps male core desires remained fixed.

Thus Ian, ranking amongst humanity's lowest common denominators, came to play an instigatory role in the mother of all plans.

Plan Bea

Part 1: The way Mammy used to make

One Bea
One Brian
One potential father-in-law
One Sunday
A scheming focused mind
A dash of spirit and *bonne chance*.
Add them together and you get Brian and Bea motoring up the M1 towards Norfolk.

'I'm nervous Brian, do I look all right?'
'Bea, don't worry.'
They were stuck in traffic, regretted not taking the train. Two hours late by the time they arrived. Brian's dad was waiting in the front garden weeding out his borders: he

waved them up the drive. It was a redbrick sash-curtained semi-detached in a redbrick sash-curtained semi-village.

There was a slap on the shoulder for Brian and a hearty handshake for Bea, a quick cup of tea, questions about the traffic and how work was progressing. Derek was a small man in his mid-sixties with an interest in model armies and he took Bea on a military tour of his prize battalions on display in mid-action. The guest room had been converted into various battlegrounds from Waterloo to the present day. In the centre of the room suspended from the lamp was a hanging missile on its way through a cardboard cutout of the streets of Baghdad.

'Very nice, Mr Martin.'

'Call me Derek.'

They drove to the nearest green belt hostelry and joined other families for a traditional Sunday pub lunch. Roast and Yorkshire pudding, crispy potatoes with Brussels sprouts and greasy carrots. It wasn't until the bread and butter pudding that Brian's dead mother made an appearance.

'Any good, son?'

'Lovely.'

'As good as your mother's?'

'Was Brian's mum a good cook?'

Brian was always so tetchy on the subject: no matter how sneaky Bea was, he refused to open up. Bea had been waiting for this information a long time, yearned to learn what she must live up to on the mothering front and there was no better place to start than the kitchen.

Domino thought processes, Bea's purpose to acquire knowledge, which food would carry Brian back to the security of childhood, comfort and subsequently to her feet. Mrs Martin was presumed to have been a marvellous cook. A kitchen raid had been envisaged. She'd taken precautions, practised a couple of dry runs back at Ruth's, had blindfolded herself to make it more realistic while Ruth held a stopwatch. The plan worked out in meticulous detail, she had come equipped, carried a pair of kid gloves in her handbag. Psychologically geared up, she planned to leave father and son to a bonding session preferably halfway through a session of *Songs of Praise*. Acting the ever so suitable Girlfriend she would offer to make tea and disappear into the kitchen. Five minutes to glean as much information as she could and your time starts now.

Cookbook targets enshrining family favourites and the kettle is filled, pages turned and the kettle is on the boil, rattling of cupboards, 'just looking for sugar, biscuits, milk . . .' excuses made in advance. Scanning through *Mrs Olson's Family Fare*, *The Housewives' Table*, *Kitchen Cuisine*, unsure exactly what to look for but would know it when she saw it. Taut with tension, fearing interruption, being foiled or worse that Mrs Martin had been one of those mothers who cooked from the heart, time sprinting onward, the kettle steaming, page corners marred by dried cake mixture, splashings of gravy . . . then and then, with less than thirty seconds on the clock, a homemade journal entitled 'My Boy Brian's Favourite Dishes' would fall open and into her hands. It wasn't stealing it was only borrowing, Derek wouldn't notice surely. Surely Derek would not notice. The first chance Bea got she would replace them. She would definitely return them. God the adrenalin was coursing through her veins and this was just thinking about it. 'Simple food for simple folk Bea, none of your cordon blue rubbish,' replied Derek. 'Good enough for us, she loved her bread and butter pudding didn't she, Brian.'

147

Bea balked, very disillusioning and after going to all that trouble. It was not on, sure anyone can make a decent bread and butter pudding. Where's the challenge in that? Cut through, her plans thwarted and her raid no longer necessary was called off, though she did offer to make tea. *Songs of Praise* had her head done in.

Part 2: Sex and the evil eye

Know thy enemies.

With the kitchen part sorted, Bea turned her attention to the 'bedroom area' or an examination of any obscene material found therein. Graham's lust for visual aids, as Bea referred to it, was in her opinion understandable seeing as Graham was a born-again Laddite. But Brian had no excuse, Brian had herself and Bea really couldn't understand the need nor the logic. In truth it churned her stomach having lived all her life in a country whose most obscene publication was *H&E*, a naturist mag and you really would have to be desperate to be turned on by that. Being a strictly male preserve the topic was not raised and Bea presumed a sizeable pile.

Thus one fine morning as Brian was busy bathing, the Irish censor in Bea came to the fore and she undertook a formidable search of Brian's room to find where he stashed his stash. Seeing as he slept on a futon, Bea went for the chest of drawers which failed to yield anything of interest, leaving the pine wardrobe as the only other option. His clothes were neatly folded in seasonal stack order and she ran her hands under the piles, then down on her hands and knees she rummaged through his shoes and at the back of the wardrobe came across an old battered cardboard box. Lifting the lid, she pandora-ed inside, found an expired membership card to the Soft Cell fan club, a stack of pictures of himself and his mother, old party invitations and a small heap of well-read glossies. Unable to resist, she snuck a peek . . . ooohhhh, slammed it shut, opened it again, got quite horny . . . oohhh. She studied the lingerie on the pages that voluntarily fell open. Brian liked reds and purples, lace and ribbons, three pages opened at crotchless corsets. Saucy devil and she smut sniggered at the thought of Brian . . . ooohh and she heard the bathroom door open and stuffed the stuff back in the box, back in the corner, her cheeks flush rushed and she said she wasn't doing anything, nothing and why was he looking at her like that.

Part 3: Countdown commencing (and a lot of effort went into making this happen)

Ruth announced she was off on a week's retreat to some Buddhist seminar place and Bea was delighted. The Grand Plan could now be safely, privately, without fear of interruption or outside forces, executed.

Bea had the flat sparkling, every particle of dust removed, every object pushed back into place, the floors scrubbed, clean sheets on the bed, candles on the table and the smell of sweet potatoes from the oven. Sweet potatoes and duckling (don't worry, she'd make sure the smell was gone by the time Ruth returned), roast aubergine stuffing with orange zested herbs, a bottle of champagne, two bottles of wine, and to finish, homemade vanilla ice-cream, apricot crumble, coffee and *petits fours*. Bea had been in the kitchen for hours, took the day off work specifically. Stockings, suspenders, a hundred quids' worth of damage to her credit card and a long afternoon in the bath erasing sensitive places of hair growth.

There was nothing more she could humanly do.

Ian's theory would be put to the test.

Brian would tumble to her, place her on a pedestal, his arms open, declaring the ultimate . . . 'Unaccustomed as I am' . . . *No, no, more romantic, start again . . .*

'Bea,' he would say, 'Bea . . .'

'Love of my life . . . adorable one . . . oh beauty most sublime' . . . *yeah that's more like it . . .*

'From the moment we met I felt an awakening in my soul, a stirring in my loins' . . . *but better take your time Brian, I'm always having to tell you to slow down . . .*

'Ah time was when my life, shrouded in darkness, when I slummer lumber existed, lacked meaning and then . . .' *what, Brian?*

'and then as a prayer answered you appeared . . .'

. . . oohh

'You taught me what it is to love' . . . *did I? did I?*

'It is you Bea, who I think of when I wake each morning, you Bea who I dream of as I drift off to sleep. The others meant nothing' . . . *Now you're talkin' . . .*

'If for a single moment I imagined I would not see you again I would gouge out my Oedipal eyes, I should wither away instantly were you ever to turn your back to me Bea Mary Josephine O'Reilly . . .' . . . *what Brian what?*

'My life is yours, do with me what you will, bind me to you legally' . . . *YES*

'Spiritually' . . . *Yes . . .*

'I love you Bea . . . eternally' *Thrice times YES.*

She could picture it so vividly, Brian on his knees,

descending mists, Leo Sayer lookalike angels, harpsichords, she was on the brink of tears, about to ruin her mascara.

'Oh Brian, Brian Martin . . .'

Wait a minute, this was Ian's theory being put to the test and the last person Bea wanted to be stuck with for the rest of her life was someone with the dis-attributes that Ian had.

And then it dawned on her.

And a draining emotion washed through her.

Good God what had she done? Bea struck by the awful reality of her situation. What if Brian actually did propose, no surely he wouldn't, what arse would succumb to such a transparent ploy as the one she was about to execute. Any self-respecting man would see right through this outrageous farce. She was kicking herself, how could she have deigned to consider anything of worth coming from the lips of such a jerkoff like Ian.

She had been treating Brian like he was some kind of reactive primate, a total ignoramus. She couldn't credit it, realised she hadn't really credited herself.

Please God Brian won't propose.

Dear God ever faithful Bea here.

I can't believe I've been such an eejit, making the worst assumptions imaginable. I just didn't stop to consider Brian as a whole human being, I mean I do want to get married but well God I want someone who's at least decent, who isn't solely dick-centric, sorry. Look if Brian does propose, well surely it would mean he was as shallow as Ian and then I just couldn't go through with it. It would shatter my whole understanding of humanity, of civilisation, of love . . . Christ God it's not as if I'm always asking favours of you and in the scheme of things it's not such a major deal and I swear to you

I'll be a better person for it. God are you listening, God . . . oh God – and she heard the key turn in the door.

Bea was in bits, she knew she would never be able to recover if he did propose, this in some warped way was a test of his integrity. 'Honey I'm home . . .'

'Brian I don't want you to say anything, I just want you to enjoy this evening.'

'Wow, Bea you look amazing.' And he flung himself on top of her.

Each course exquisite, each course physically interrupted, on course and turning over, about to fall asleep Brian said,

'Bea.'

'What?'

'You didn't have to.'

'I know.'

'Bea . . . ?'

'What?'

'There's something I want to ask you.'

'Don't say it Brian, please don't say it. I'm tired, talk to me tomorrow.'

'No I want to ask you now.'

'Brian, I'm knackered. Tomorrow.'

'Bea, the meal was amazing.'

'Thanks, night.'

'Sex incredible.'

'Night, Brian.'

'Bea, I don't know how to say this.'

'Then don't.'

'Bea, is there someone else?'

He thought she was eliminating a guilty conscience.

'Come here you big woofter,' says herself and she rolled over to him. 'Gis a kiss.'

Making tracks

A book of evidence lay open on a leather-topped desk, faint thumbprints on the corner of page XXIV. Adam perched on the edge of a high-backed chair, sitting forward, strumming his fingers on the woodstained surface. CC was at reception. His client waiting for him. He rose from his seat, his spirits risen, the temperature rising, summer already. Spring around the corner and the occasion had sprung upon him. Had taken him by surprise, penetrated his routine and left him thinking of possibilities.

Something happened and yet . . . he woke with a sore head alone . . . and yet nothing occurred. He remembered that much. Fluently, fluidly conversing without having to think of what was coming next. Adam thought of her body encased in his, wrapped around her fingers. An unusual encounter, a chemical reaction, a lingering narcotic and rapid thought rushes streamed through his consciousness, of her, of her, of perhaps being with her.

He had taken a chance, when he should have been with friends drinking designer beers, eyeing up fancified women, enjoying that almost obligatory outing to mark the beginning of each sacred weekend. He had sought sanctuary, found it one evening when he stopped by a pub promising nothing, ordered a drink from the bar and started doing a crossword.

Of course she had behaved impeccably, left before his eyes opened, avoided the morning-after embarrassment. That woeful feeling, the hanging continuum when you want to flee, when the strangeness of the face lying beside you takes on horrific proportions. The previous night's bullshitting so visible in unkind morning light and you realise you're safer on your own. Too much effort entailed in opening up. No need to open up. No marks left. Intriguingly attractive. She was so attractive. No sign of her visit bar a picture in the living room, displaced, no forwarding number, just tracks in the dust on the shelf.

Adam stood at the office window. Stood sniffling, a fine line of dust on the window ledge, static traffic below impatient to move on.

A judgment looming, drawing near, the hacks beginning to stir. The usual story, boy meets girl.

On that precise evening a crack had appeared in Adam's ordered life, a moment of potential chaos and his mind kept straying from the case. Indeed a fence was being erected ensuring both sides had somewhere to stand, there would be no crossing the lines of play. It was all down to strategy. A victim compliant, an attempt to frame his client, the assassination of a hapless character for the price of fame in a tabloid tissue.

Atishoo, Atishoo, hay fever spreading like pollen as lawns are cut and dust begins to dry-ride across the city.

She was out there, anywhere, at any time he might bump into her again, and he wondered what his chances were. He kept her in his mind, forcibly retaining her there, ah and it's a dangerous thing to do, chaste escapism, your own little lie but hours pass by sweeter and dreams come alive. Head creations, what the eye don't see and it reminded Adam of a time back then when magic existed.

Child time, when the imagination is revered and you can talk to yourself without fear of internment. Your own special friend. He caught Ben at it, a reflecting mirror bringing him back to childhood like a wafting smell and suddenly you're somewhere else and age melts. A child's measure of time, ever in the present, no thought of repercussions, of boundaries. He heard his voice chattering lightly. The door to Ben's room slightly ajar and he stood outside spying, unseen.

He missed the sound of Ben's small voice and the morning heat of his body lying next to his. The telling and retelling of Chicken Licken and Henny Penny. That was the worst part. Hayley could leave him and she did, she did and she took Ben with her. It hadn't mattered: Ben was not his child, he hoped they would have another child, a child of their own. Hayley kept putting it off. Her job taking her across the world and back, across the world . . . eight years, a long time in a child's life, in his life.

People adapt to pain, become immune after a while, the courts were full of them. Then you move swiftly on and you pick up the pieces and after a time it doesn't feel so raw.

By morning light she fled.

Her face familiar, Adam was sure he'd seen her before . . . it would come to him. He had a good memory for faces. The sound of revving engines, impatient to move along . . . move along, red light looming like a red . . . it would come to him. He was positive he had seen her before.

Peering down at the traffic through the slits in the office blinds, the lights turned green and cars edged slowly forward. It may have been a trick of the light for she had evaporated into thin air, could be near, could be so close by.

He retraced his tracks, backtracked to the dingy pub just in case, in case . . .

The office door opened and CC was shown in.

'CC' – Adam stretched out his hand – 'Good to see you.' Adam indicated to the chair facing his own.

Unsettling news, a potential hitch had CC frowning.

'I haven't received all the details yet, CC.'

'So out of the blue someone has come forward?'

'I shouldn't worry too much.'

'But you're saying I should worry, a little.'

'I just want to keep you aware of all the facts.'

Adam ran his fingers through his hair. Piles of paper on his desk, accumulating evidence, obscuring reality where black fades to white like . . . like magic, one minute she's there and the next she's gone.

Baby Bea

On her marks . . . at a set of traffic lights . . . the green man flashing . . . go Bea go. But in two minds whether to cross or wait, cross or wait, Bea dithered. She'd have to make a dash, was wearing high heels, clodhoppers, plod plodders to walk tall whilst maintaining a balance, she might trip in haste and then she would end up splat just like Gat . . . Road rules remembered, Green Cross Code, you got a Brownie badge if you passed, Bea still had hers somewhere. 'Bea,' hollered from the other side, 'Bea' mouth cupped shouted, waving her forward, magnetic tones, drawing her over, *when I'm calling youououououououo . . .*

Hesitation, hesitation, forfeit two points and with zero seconds left she chased the green man to the other side.

Made it –

well you've got to take a few risks in life.

'Bea, how are you?'

Puffing, panting and she really shouldn't have given up aerobics.

Donald . . . Donald . . . ? He was looking different.

'What do you think? Fancied a change, it's all the rage.' He was referring to his hair, he'd turned platinum blond.

'Very in your face, Donald.'

'And you're looking gorgeous, Bea.' Flirt, flirt always the charmer.

Flustered flustered, flattered flustered, red cheek blusher, the cheek of him, why did he holler, nearly had her run over, her heart dancing and a snatched synopsis of the past few months . . .

'Do you have time for a coffee, Bea?'

'Can't, sorry, I'm . . . busy.' Busy Bea and she was taken aback, caught unawares. He said he'd call her.

'Great, OK, whatever.'

Weird.

Donald, weird, Donald Donald swimming around in her head. Why so now, just when she'd managed to let go . . . go away . . . away with you and some people have that disconcerting knack of nude nerve touching. Donald was one such. Bea thought she had de-systemised him from out of her. Thought she had scraped the last Donald remains away.

Bastard.

He'd knocked the stuffing from her, there was no doubting that. She had pushed it aside, to be dealt with later. Refused to think about it. Refuse . . . bastard.

Shit double shit.

Donald Double Trouble.

Shitty Shitty clang bang . . . too many things left unsaid.

A primary school at the end of Bea's road, a daily wade through a shoal of short grey trousers, black blazers, tiny ties (probably elastic), porky pies and shrill voices. Then quiet, the school gong, clang banging, shit double shit, scarper . . .

'cause the hooked nosed child sniffer snatcher in his gaudily disguised ice-cream van, back bent over was ringing his tinkle bell. Donald said he would ring. Summer and the school bereft of babelings and suddenly the playground is ominously bare.

Bea had sensed she was pregnant before she had a chance to miss a period, her tits felt uniquely sensitive. Donald had left her with a micro reminder, a going away present of the potentially lasting sort. What surprised Bea most was her reaction, her cool rationality. This was not part of the plan. How did it happen? She had always tried to be careful, she did try, OK so she'd skipped a pill or two, or three. Hell, it happens. Christ the last thing she had foreseen was bringing a child up alone.

Pissing over a pregnancy tester, warm orange pee cascading through her fingers, turning white to pink and the outcome known. An appointment was booked, a couple of days taken off work and Bea had gone on auto-trau-matic. Didn't tell anyone, not a whisper to anyone, her mother would have been destroyed, would have destroyed her. How could you? how could you? It was nobody's business, a cluster of cells in the wrong place at the wrong time, it was an accident, over in a couple of hours, gone. It was so easy, she hardly felt a thing, matter of fact.

Substance, matter, it hadn't really happened, got lost in a vacuum of subconsciousness. Donald's reaction was not sought, she knew it would be negative. He would accuse her of planning it, as if she would do something like that to entrap him, or he would deny it . . . it just didn't bear thinking about, not when she had to deal with 'it'.

From deep inside her a strength surfaced and she had followed her instinct. This time Bea trusted herself, no questions asked, no dithering.

All in good time, revenge promised and if the opportunity should ever arise Bea had sworn on a life to hurt Donald. Indeed it would all come out in the wash and if she got the chance she would like to hand back some of the hurt he'd been so generous with. Proof of purchase in her filofax in the form of a hospital receipt.

A new man in her life, a new brand of contraceptive, Bea and Brian, their regular soap opera evening and they'd been bickering about Single Mothers.

Bea had proclaimed her disgust towards such wanton women in right-wing terminology. 'Enforced abortion it's the only answer. Every pregnant woman should be means tested, if she can't afford to have a kid then she shouldn't have a kid, believe me Brian there's enough bastards in the world already.'

'You're telling me you'd abort a baby.'

Bea didn't answer.

She lost control to her emotions, her lips trembled precariously, her nostrils flared. Remorse was such a crap word and choice is such a vicious thing. A luxury. As if, what choice had she and she screamed at Brian to answer her. What choice had she? what choice? She demanded an answer.

'None, Bea,' and Brian held her tight to stop her quaking shaking, her emotion motion and he thumb-wiped tears away and he told he loved her. She sobbed so much, the next day she had to wear shades to work. Her eyes red wired swollen.

In a kind attempt to cheer her up Brian sent a bouquet of flowers to the office which sparked another dose of saline droplets to cloud Bea's vision.

Donald called.

He said he'd been thinking about her a lot, couldn't wait to see her again. He asked if they could meet in the little café where they used to spend Sunday mornings, that is when he bothered to come home of a Saturday night. Bea was angry, red sore angry, made him grovel, granted his request on condition they met during lunch hour at a crap sandwich bar near her office. She never mentioned it to Brian, it concerned herself, Donald and an unspoken matter.

Late and looking her best, Bea pushed the café door open, the bell tinkled.

Child snatcher. It takes two to tango to share the guilt, the shame.

Donald was waiting for her at a table by the window, he watched her come in, good to see you girl, he was finding it hard to suppress a smile.

'Donald.'

'Bea.'

'Cup of tea?'

'I didn't think you were going to show.'

'I'm going to get something to eat, do you want anything?'

Armour intact Bea ordered a pastrami and coleslaw sandwich. Matters would be conducted in a businesslike manner. There would be no surrender, Bea was dressed in Paisley's colours. She was staying with her English man and would not capitulate to the charms of her ex. No way, no how, no never, she'd been humming 'God Save the Queen' all morning.

He told her things were going fine, he was a freelance journalist now, all that hard work paid off, he was making money, being paid for what he always wanted to do.

'And you know what, Bea?'

'What?'

He says it means nothing, he'd made a mistake, these people he'd always aspired to be like, to work with were shallow, superficial. It's all talk, pure front, game playing, a game of words on paper for a weekly pay cheque, writing rubbish to fill in column space . . .

'Bullshit Bea, honestly, I'm so disillusioned, guess you were right, I've been a fool.'

His life was lacking in substance. Donald was after some integrity.

'Crissy's dumped me.'

Really? and that did surprise Bea, the model girl must have had some brain cells, what goes around . . . poor Donald, substance lacking plus a battered ego. Life sucks sometimes, doesn't it?

So tail between his thighs, big boy Donald wants love. Wants affection. Did he think she was that easy? the click of his fingers and she'd come running . . . across a road.

Did he actually believe all he had to do was call out her name and hey presto . . . crossroads.

'Come to cry on my soft shoulders have you?'

'Bea don't be like that.'

Oh he changed course pretty quick, she saw right through him, good old reliable Bea, ever at the ready with emotional support.

'You'll just have to get over her, Donald, believe me you will.'

'How long has it been, Bea?'

He probably expected her to know the hours, the minutes, the seconds and she did but she wasn't going to say.

'Come back to me, Bea.'

Funny how not so long ago she would have paid him to consider what he had just said. She wasn't laughing. He disgusted her, his mind games misfiring, still thinks I'm his, still thinks he has control.

'Donald you're grasping at straws, you never really loved me.'

'But we were good together, Bea.'

'Nah. I was good to you.'

Playing pathetic, plain pathetic.

'I'm sorry Bea.' He slid his hand across the table.

He was reaching out, hoping she would take his palm in her hand and give him some psychic comfort.

Fool.

A hospital bill lay stuffed inside her filofax, swimming along with her lipstick, purse, keys, and empty chocolate wrappers.

163

She listened as he renounced his wicked ways. He hadn't changed, sought redemption from the dependable one.

'I can't believe I treated you so badly, Bea.'

'I let you treat me like that.'

'I'm broke, Bea, freelancing and the cheque is always in the post.'

Incredible: only ten minutes ago his life had been dandy, his visible ulterior motives definitely lacking in charm.

'So you're skint?'

He didn't want to ask, not outright, he hated to ask but she was his only friend.

Bea rummaged in her bag, Donald thought she was going for her purse.

A filofax raised, flicking through it. Donald thought it must be a note, ten, twenty, he knew she wouldn't let him down.

'Donald I never told you this.'

She was looking at the receipt, it was folded in four.

'God Bea, thanks a lot I knew you'd pull through.'

Pull through? Yeah I did no thanks to you, what difference if she showed him the physical scar. He still couldn't contemplate anything beyond his own ego.

He hadn't even asked her how she was.

Her filofax clasped shut, the red-inked paper inside. Her anger subsiding, her hurt scabbed over. She was feeling strong. Bea had moved on, she had, since their split, definitely moved on. Words left unarticulated there was no point no more.

Bea rose from the chair, gathered her belongings.

'What are you doing, Bea?'

'Shit Donald I've got to go.'

'What about the money I . . .'

'I thought you didn't like to ask.'

'Yeah but.'

'So don't. Take care of yourself Donald, hope things work out.'

She left him bewildered, milking sympathy from a mug of tea.

Deep Bea breathing and she felt so good. It was a beautiful day. The sun was out, was shining down on her face, her sun dappled freckled face. Her bag swung lightly at her side and with a certain spring in her step she made her way to work.

Seeing the woods from the trees

Up on Parliament Hill, the whole of London at my feet, an unblemished view of a blemished city on a summer hot day. A cooling breeze laps at bare legs, winds its way around calves and further to tease my heat. Sat on a bench, thinking, accumulating bench marks, lashes against the back of my thighs. The second millennium in view and I can see far from the top of this hill. The air is better up here, the air is much clearer, much better, down below my lungs clog up. I have become saturated by filth, heavy with waste. You can travel far if your direction is focused so I walked the streets of London up to Parliament Hill, to a paint-peeling bench and watched kite flyers take off. The unfettered sun rode the sky, no strings attached turned the heavens blue, demolishing cloud storms and I was sure I was going to cry. I felt a load on my mind but the heat stroked me calm and melted head knots. I was breathing steady, heavy, losing my self behind multicoloured eyelids. I didn't notice his presence at first.

Little lost boy, boy blue wandering fields far from home sat at the far end of the bench. A school satchel over his shoulders, snivelling, lollipop licking, snot drop melting sugared water, his knees grazed grit studded.

'Are you all right?' I asked.

'I'm running away.'

'Where are you going?'

'Nowhere.'

'Where did you come from?'

'Nowhere.'

'What are you doing out on your own?'

'Nothing.'

'How old are you?'

'Seven and a half.'

He threw the licked stick on to the grass, sweet orange puddled on his tiny thigh, he dipped his finger in then licked it. Loose limbs, perfectly formed, his feet not touching the earth. No icepop stick jokes any more, no more lolli laughs.

He wiped his eyes with the back of his hands and I offered him a hanky.

'No thanks.'

He was only small, browned off face and pudding bowl hair.

'Were you in a fight?'

'Maybe – it's not fair,' he said.

'What?'

He wasn't listening, he was working things out in his head.

He had lost his key, was a latch key kid, his mother had tied it around his neck. He had got into a scrap, a scrap attack.

'Women,' he said

He was ambushed back there and he pointed to a far field in the distance. Long grass waving up at us.

'I fought them off'

and he raised his eyes, the youth of today. Barely out of nappies and already fighting. They had stolen his latch key, mistook it for the key to his heart.

'They are always doing that,' I said. 'I guess you had a narrow escape.'

He knows more than he will ever know, he is pure and uncomplicated, clear crystal clear, his skin is soft and beautiful, so new.

'So little man with the world on your shoulders would you like to come back to my place?'

'My mother told me never to solicit strangers.'

'Look Mister I'm only trying to help.'

'Talking to strangers is forbidden.'

I resented that. I was not a stranger, I may be strange but I really am not a stranger and I took out my wallet, my red plastic wallet to prove to the boy I did exist and I told him I would compromise myself if he didn't trust me.

Little Mister, an uncorrupted version of his elders, innocence incarnate with my good self. I wanted to touch him. He was seven years old enough to know better, young enough to run. He was smaller than I, maybe it was a youth thing. I wanted to have him before the others got their greasy hands on him and ruined him and destroyed any goodness inside. I wanted to have first crack at the whip.

'I want to show you something.'

'Sweets is it?'

A gift-carrying goddess for my little messiah. I could have had him, manipulated him. Ipulated my little man.

'Trying to buy me off, lady?'

I am no lady, Mister, should you care to come back to my place I can show you a thing or two. If you follow my lead I will take you to a lovely place and we can dress up. I'll put on a suit, an expensive suit. Tailored to fit like a glove. Very nice. You can wear something colourful and pretty. I'll even buy it for you, whatever you want and we can pretend we're grown up . . . I was getting carried away, sinful yearnings of a priestly kind, a shudder ran me through. Grounded me, he was only a babe, I would have crushed him, pipsqueaked him. Christ what was I thinking. I was thinking I was young once too.

No no much better if I tell you a story, really I just wanted to tell you a story. There is no need to fear me, I couldn't hurt you if I wanted to, honestly, promise, promise, cross my heart, hope to die, I swore on my life.

He nudged over close, the pause between us narrowed and he asked me to tell him a story.

Once upon a time in the land of the little people there lived a tiny tot. She was so small, she hardly existed. We shall call her Non for short. One day when summer was calling, Non was brought on a school outing to a place called Bray. It is an old seaside resort about fifteen miles south of the city of Dublin. Hardly a paradise quite shabby even then having fallen from grace due to the rise of the motor car. Anyhow the beach was wide and long but it was pebbly. Not a grain of sand in sight and there was a raised promenade, huge slabs of paving stones with blue rusty railings running the length of the strand and at the very end of the beach there were amusement arcades, tucked beneath a small mountain or perhaps a large hill and perched on the top was a huge looming cross.

Jesus was crucified for us. I used to cry about Jesus. He wasn't one for shying away, nor for modesty come to think of it, naked save for a patch of iron cloth. There he was up on Bray Head nailed to his crucifix. Poor bloke out in all types of weather looking down upon us. Jesus wept but he'd move a man of stone to tears, cross my heart hope to die, where was I, yes, yes, that's it, way down at the far end of the beach, a speck of dust in the eyes of our Lord. It's just a story, honestly.

We disembarked, the school bus parked as far as the eye can see, in the furthermost car park from the arcades which were to be our final goal. The amusement arcades, a yardstick to keep us in line.

And ordered to line up we were, a trail of uniformed children wound its way down to the beach. We had brought packed lunches to eat on tartan patterned picnic rugs laid out for our comfort. Socks and shoes, brown lace-ups removed and we went to paddle in the sea, skim stones upon the waves, stones thrown, Fido flung sticks and names shall never hurt.

Such a good girl.

But are you the best?

Shure I am Mister, shure I am.

Balls thrown in play and I'm jesting I'm jesting . . . in rhythm with its bounce and I'm playing I'm playing,

. . . A my name is Annabel my husband's name is Arthur we live in Arklow and we sell apples. Shiny red apples.

The ball bouncing off the paving stones tapping the underside of my hand, tapping me on the head –

The prettiest girl in the world.

From the ground to my hands, hands to the ground, up . . . down . . . up . . . down . . . a rubber ball with colours inside, lots of bounce.

We had moved from the beach, rugs rerolled and under arms. On our way to the arcade.

In retrospect he was very underhand.

Bouncing to the arcade,

. . . B my name is Betty my husband's name is Bernard we live in Booterstown and we sell balls . . .

There were bumper cars and a waltzer and a ghost train and we were to stick together and not run off.

. . . C my name is Catriona, my husband's name is Colm we live in Coolock . . . Damnit and the ball bounced askew, ricocheted off a misplaced pebble. Rolled away, out of reach, out of line, I was out of line, chasing a roll away, kicked by a misplaced foot, rolled further, under there, where? under hand and I ran to retrieve it, to start again,

. . . A my name is Angela, my husband's name is Ardal we live in Africa and we sell . . .

He had a shiny red toffee apple and was holding it out, tempting me. A red shiny toffee apple, worth a million dollars in childhood currency. I'd do anything to get it, anything. I was standing beside the Laughing Policeman. He'd make you chuckle. We'd drop our pennies in, chink, chink and the mechanical keeper of the peace would start laughing his head off. You could hear him from the far corner of the arcade, away from the machines, you could still hear him then. But he wasn't a real guard, a 'Garda', he was an outdated 'RIC' boxed up after Independence. See he never made it to the rescue. His arms would chug in and out, bent at the elbows, his bulgy cheeks rouged and hard with a truncheon in one hand.

He held his truncheon in his hand and I had a sticky face.

Sugared face, sticky red apple in my hand, some things just cloy to your memory and it was taken off me.

Goddamnit but I had earned that fucking apple.

No one else in the group was allowed sticky faces from shiny red . . . I wasn't either. It was taken off me. Fair is fair. One minute you're as good as gold, the next minute you're bad as sin and the Laughing Policeman ran out of gas.

'Is that it?' asked the boy.

'Yeah what do you think?'

'Not much of a story.'

I apologised, it was the first thing that came to mind.

'Nothing about running away in it either.'

'That came later, much later but the moral is . . .'

There must be a moral for I surely couldn't have gone through the whole episode for nothing '. . . always stick to lollies.'

He asked me if I would walk him home, the sun was embered out, the day lagging, he said the park was full of weirdos and I seemed like a nice one.

Best of the lot and I took his hand and he led me down through the heath.

Bea's BBQ

Brian and Bea invite you, oh you lucky thing, you specially picked upon person . . . hey remember school, remember standing in line waiting to be chosen by one of the team captains and being the last one picked, the odd one out, when did you ever get the chance to be a team captain? . . . and hey hey if you did, you'd show them . . . wouldn't you . . . **to their Summer BBQ** celebrating moving in together and choice of habitat.

It really is a super duper flat, oh pardonnez moi did I say flat?

Terribly sorry meant apartment. And hasn't Bea done well, isn't it all so cosy, note the curtains aren't nets, no fake plastic flowers in the windows or blue-collar ornaments, sheer sophistication, sheer je ne sais quoi . . .

On Friday August 30th – Remember to bring a bottle, and a decent bottle what's more, none of your cheap plonk picked up in a Paki store on the way over, as Bea undoubtedly will have spent the whole day working her sweet flabby ass off for your benefit, marinating fresh fish, expensive fish like salmon, tuna and king prawns, not to mention free range chicken and lamb kebabs the like of which you won't be getting at any Tom Dick or Harry BBQ. Of course if you're vegetarian, Bea is sure to have prepared some mouthwatering delicacy, rest assured your every need will have been catered for. This shall be no ordinary do, oh no, we will be graced by the presence of a chosen few. The most hip trendy people available to Bea via Brian: producers, directors, important PAs, lovely people, glad to make your acquaintance people and of course models, well one at least, oh do mind your dribbles, these people have lives, these people are important.

Bea is becoming her mother. Any normal mother would hand a stack of cards to the teacher who duly handed them out to each pupil. Bea's mother wasn't having any of that, oh no, only girls whose parents were prosperous or influential were asked. My inclusion was due to my father's membership of a certain exclusive golf club which Bea's dad was trying to get sponsored for. I can see it now, weighed down in a maxi dress and playing musical statues for the nth time.

'Now we are going to have a *wonderful* afternoon, play lots of *nice* games and then *funny* Mr Punch is coming to entertain us.' Christ the woman was so patronising.

Bea's seventh b-day, sixteen bibbed girlies sat stoic round a table full of iced buns, Krispie cakes, egg sandwiches, and marshmallows dipped in chocolate with Smarties stuck on top. An edible Jemima (of *Play School* fame) ablaze prompting us to chant the birthday melody and illuminating a small writhing heap in the arms of Bea's father. It was Bea's younger 'physically challenged' brother. The lights were off so only a few observant kiddies noticed. He was mentally gone too, unaware he was the hidden child, the quirk in Mrs Bea's genetic history. I've never liked Bea's mother, she has never liked me, due in part to the incident that was to follow.

The concluding cries of 'so say all of us' hollered forth

with birthday sincerity and as Bea blew out the candles little brother was whisked out of sight, wish time and Bea opted for a tadpole, in the hope that one day he might grow up to be a frog and then he might even grow up to be a prince. I asked why didn't she just wish for a prince and she got into a huff and refused to let me play Pass the Parcel.

So I went to make a more detailed examination of Bea's weird sibling. I put it down to childish inquisitiveness, another odd one out, a kindred spirit and I swear to you I thought I was doing him a favour. He looked so uncomfortable, so contorted so I held him by his feet, was trying to stretch out his twisted limbs, had him upside down when Mrs O'Reilly suddenly appeared in the doorway. Surprised me, bouncity bounce and I dropped the kid on his head. Mrs O'Reilly's nerves got the better of her and for my antics she gave me a clout round the earhole which I considered unjustly deserved and kicked her back in the shins. Look the damage was already done, if she hadn't butted in I'm sure I would have replaced him right side up. For the rest of the party I was ostracised, no going home pressie for me and Mrs O'Reilly called my parents, requiring my immediate removal from her premises. I was never formally asked to Bea's again.

So a letter pops through the box with an RSVP which I didn't reply to, guess I've been feeling kinda excluded of late, followed by a phone call.

'Are you over the moon for me, are you? are you?' triumphant Bea informing me of her up and coming cohabiting status. 'I'm almost there.'

175

I applaud you dear Bea, just what you always wanted, weighted limbs and a constantly suspicious mind.

'Wonderful and how did all this transpire?'

'How could he resist.'

Easily, no I am truly glad and she told me about their flat-hunting escapade.

'Yeah I noticed the address part was omitted.'

At . . . To Be Advised

'We haven't found a place yet.'

'It's two weeks away.'

'I know, but I have faith. We're seeing a penthouse this evening.'

I guess she meant a top-floor flat.

And two weeks later I found myself being led through a loft like but comfortable apartment, somewhere near Islington which Bea assures me is actually the 'in place' of the borough. Indeed they have the top floor and they have a roof terrace. She really has surpassed herself.

I was relegated with the not so cool, the people you have to invite no matter what.

'I'll catch up with you later, got to look after my guests,' and Bea made a beeline.

Oh for God's sake where's old bumbling Bea, do you not remember those Soho Boho nights of lore, fixing you up with any dick that would rise to the occasion.

Bea's gone all level headed and I can't cope with it. Scoop of the century and the woman is almost fluorescent, herself and Brian, living in harmony as one.

And I notice she's put on a little weight. Maybe it's that lookalike Laura Ashley dress, that whiff of domesticity, the ribbon in her hair, just remember kiddo you haven't made it to suburbia yet.

Throat dry with envy I poured myself a hefty double vodka.

Bea stood uncorking a bottle of white wine, surveying the situation. How utterly wonderful, magical. A clear summer evening, Brian at her side and their lovely guests mingling effortlessly. Sighs of satisfaction and in Bea's wildest dreams she never actually believed all would work as graphically plotted. Her conniving scheming ways surely had no influence on events and she opted to shift the responsibility on to the will of our Lord. It was Graham's doing really, fast declining he had given up on the job front and taken to slobbery as a full-time occupation. More than a bad influence Graham had become a source of interference in Bea and Brian's quality time together and smelling disaster Bea took the initiative, offering him her services as personal careers guide.

'A hunting we will go, Graham,' crooned Bea, flicking the jobs section of the paper in his face. Bea helped him with applications, calmed him down before interviews, brought him shopping for a new suit and what kind of thanks did she get? . . . More than enough, she got rid of him.

Graham had of late received news that a position applied for had been granted and a good job would be transporting him to Manchester.

'The jammiest jam job in the universe, and we're all going out to get smashed,' cheered Graham, the financial analyst, the best goddamn analyst in the world and his ego hit the ceiling and stuck there like an Olympic wanker's winning entry.

'Brian, I'm going to rent the place out, you and Bea have first refusal.'

'Refused, and don't give Bea any big ideas.'

However it was in his own cavernous brain that the idea rested and the teeny tiny possibility of his moving out of Graham's and in with Bea began to find expression.

Bea: 'Brian what are you going to do?'
Brian: 'I don't know.'
Bea: 'Brian what are you going to do?'
Brian: 'I don't know.'
Bea: 'Brian what are you going to do?'
Brian: 'I don't know.'
Bea: 'Brian what are you going to do?'
Brian: 'Maybe we should get a place together.'
Bea: 'We'll have to see about that. I'm pretty comfortable here with Ruth.'

Over the following weeks, what with Graham's departure imminent and strangers being shown around the flat, Brian finally came to the conclusion that it was imperative Bea and himself move in together, his argument supported by a list kindly compiled by herself.

Brian's List – The pros and cons on sharing with Bea

For	*Or*
Less expensive	Exorbitant
Bea	No Bea, lonely-depressed
Lots of sex	Less sex
Bea's cooking	Take-outs

No Ruth	Ruth
Less travelling expenses to see Bea	Travelling expenses to see Bea
Nice flat	Dingy hole
No Bea phone bill	Massive phone bill
Everyone else lives with their boyfriend/girlfriend	Lonely, sad thirty-three-year-old
Fun	No fun

Together they plotted, north of the river or south of the river, Hackney, Battersea, Ladbroke Grove? Primrose Hill? Hampstead? Decisions, decisions and they wanted space, they wanted a garden, they wanted it all. Then a friend of a friend who was going to live in China for a year, offered them his top-floor flat on condition they looked after his cats. The Berians expressed their interest in all things feline and a deal was struck.

Everything worked out grand, Bea's fourth jotter complete. They were fast tracking up the matrimonial path, a flat, a pet. Ten out of ten, time to party.

Brian suggested a house warming, social lubrication to mark his passage from bachelordom. He was fairly relieved to be moving out: mate loyalty and sheer laziness had kept Brian put, it was always such a hassle to move. On this occasion he left it to Bea, departed Clapham one fine morning, did a day's work and arrived in Islington to find the transition complete.

Brian had been thinking his mother would have liked Bea. Bea. Soft skinned and peachy. Cuddly and warm. Plump yet sexy. And nice with it, no airs and graces. Bea had depth and width. Ordinary – she was ordinary, open and friendly. With Bea, he could cut the bullshit to a minimum. She had an aura of comfort about her, an inner confidence, knew her own mind. Brian liked that, he liked strong women.

Brian had a plan. It was formulating in his head: a company of his own. He'd mentioned it in passing to a blue chip client whom he got on really well with, realised he had enough pulling power and hoped to strike out solo by the end of the year. Bea would support him, he didn't doubt it; if he played his cards right her folks might even invest some capital.

The BBQ was their first joint venture and he watched Bea mesmerised by her party planning strategies. It had started with a list of twenty-six potentials, whittled down to twenty-five after some ritual argy-bargying. Top of the list were Brian's work associates, followed by those he wanted to work with. It was crucial to have the right mix of people and Bea made him invite his friend Adam. The CC Arles case was back in the news, trial time in a couple of days. Bea was sure everyone would be dead interested. Brian's list came to twenty-two and Bea mustered the remaining three.

She had organised the party to incorporate three distinct social pivotal points to encourage mingling.

The BBQ and himself were positioned in one corner equidistant from a table resplendent with buffet type offerings (salads, three-leaf lettuce, buffalo tomato and mozzarella, mixed, etc.) and the drinks were placed in the kitchen. There was a sprinkling of night lights scattered to enhance the atmosphere, and Ruth came early so no one had to suffer first-guest syndrome. Bea hoped for a fluid evening with lots of chatter, she said she wanted the sound of laughter ringing in her ears. Brian's hopes were more humble and he aimed to get wrecked and have a good time.

By nine o'clock the coals were smouldering and a fine smell of charred prawns wafted. Brian was brushing excess marinade over the meat in earshot of Bea who was cracking him up, she was practising her official hostess demeanour:

'Great to see you.' 'You look marvellous.' 'Stoke Newington, but that's ages away!'

'Very Thai-ian' declared Jay Goldsworthy, making an entrance, attempting to grab as much attention as possible and succeeding.

'What an arse,' sighed Bea, cringing as Jay scoffed four king-size prawns in a row, undoing in an instant a vital part of her party planning. Four king-size prawns, a sixth of all prawns. Bea had entertained the hope that each of her guests would get a fair share.

To her left a group of Brian's would-be associates were chatting:

'What are you up to later?'

'Nick's having a party, d'you fancy it?'

Jesus Mary, they had only arrived and already they were talking about leaving. Bea's smile broadened with tension and she looked to her right. A couple were sitting uncomfortably, the girl smoking and the guy telling her about a film by a certain Peruvian director, whose name he couldn't remember: 'You know the one I mean.' While his girlfriend insistently replied, 'I don't'.

Relax Bea, relax, the party was only warming up and though Bea's smile was in the process of straightening out, her inner voice kept her calm, this party is, is going to be a success. It bloody well is. She poured some wine into a proffered glass.

'There you go, Adam. Such a shame CC couldn't come.'

It was a fine evening stemming from an over-hot day when Londoners sweat and complain about the weather, how stifling it is and how air conditioning should be made compulsory. I was stuck in the nobs' corner with Ruth and Graham, the latter was on to me like a sexual disease, the former a death sentence.

'Hiya.'

'Hi Ruth.' We passed shallow phrases ringing empty and a great big spliff ringing true. She was blocking my view to all those really important people, but hey who gives a shit when there's smoke in your lungs.

Then Ruth asks me if I had heard of Tantric sex: 'I've been seeing this counsellor for the past four weeks and I can tell you I'm a changed person.'

And I'm thinking that's a relief, had thought I was going to be bored shitless.

'Have you ever seen a counsellor?'

'No Ruth I haven't.'

'Oh you should, it's very good.'

Ruth's talk was most intriguing and Graham was in on it like a shot. Anything to do with sex attracted him like a shit to flies being one of those poor blokes who can't communicate with women unless his knob end has a chance of getting sticky. Everything he says includes or is a derivative allusion to copping off.

182

'It's about the coming together of two people on a spiritual plane, a thunderous orgasmic experience of a quality I had not even fantasised about.'

'I hope you're talking about me,' Graham butted in.

'No I was talking about my therapist.'

'Eh, what's this then?'

'He believes sex is interrelated with our whole being and only by expressing ourselves physically can we ever really be free.'

'So like you're paying some geezer to have sex with you?'

'It's not like that at all, it's pure, sacred.'

Poor Ruth, poor deluded Ruth as desperate as any of us really.

Graham was getting overheated.

'Do you ever have group sessions?'

'Well actually we are having one next week.'

Ruth described in scantily clad detail the upcoming event where she would be getting physical with at least four others, assuring us it wouldn't be sordid or vulgar.

'In fact Malcolm said he would videotape it so no one in the future could claim he was being morally unethical.'

She said this with a straight face.

I excused myself, went to refill my glass.

Brian and Bea may have a rooftop terrace but the skyline didn't amount to much. It wasn't Paris by any stretch of the imagination and I closed my eyes to test this theory.

'It's not exactly Paris.' Words unrushed falling from lips dry.

'Hey Mister are you reading my thoughts?'

183

Well, well, and what do you know, he was standing at my side again, my crossword puzzler. It is such a rare thing to bump into someone in this great grand city. Chances are one in 78,462 with a margin of error. Maybe I'm wrong, maybe I don't look hard enough. I pass a million lives, moving in different directions, no communication and for days on end speak to no one. Not a soul, not a single solitary conversation to pass the time of day with. Coincidence or part of a greater plot, will you shatter into thousands of pieces, drift away as early morning dew or will . . .

He lit a cigarette and leant over the rail close beside me, his jacket touching my bare arm.

'You didn't leave a number.'

'I . . .'

Bea rushed over, interrupting us:

'Adam's a solicitor, he's working on the CC Arles case.'

I started to cough, splutter. Guess my drink went down the wrong way.

'Are you OK?'

My voice cracking up and Bea drags me off to get some water.

'Nice, isn't he?'

'I've met him before.'

'Oh that's a coincidence, you never mentioned it.'

Brian strolled over, handed me an overdone drumstick which had been ignored by everyone else.

'We haven't seen much of you lately.'

'Oh you know how it is Brian, best friend falls in love and disappears off the face of the earth.'

'All my fault and now you hate me.'

'No Brian I've always hated you.'

We laughed, rolled a mighty jay and I pulled Ruth away

from Graham, asked her to elaborate further on her therapy session and we laughed some more. For all Brian's shortcomings he has a wicked sense of humour. It was cruel but funny.

Adam having worked late was in desperate need of some light entertainment. He remembered Brian's message on his answerphone and decided to go, there was nothing on TV, anyhow it was far too nice to be staying indoors.

'The thing is the middle classes are becoming increasingly docile and the poor dull in the extreme. Jay Goldsworthy.' Jay took Adam by the hand, a firm grasp, she was a very forthright person.

'One would think with the millennium just around the corner there'd be a continuous spate of revolts, rebellions, revolutions. Are you married?'

'Divorced.' As divorced as he was from this conversation.

Funny that, meeting her again. Nice funny and he watched her from afar. She caught him and smiled. A wide, deep smile and he wondered if like himself she had held on to that night. He was glad he'd decided to come.

Jay rattled on:

'The whole fabric of society is threadbare. The result being no doubt a sociopolitical crisis on a scale complementary to its historical context.'

'I don't understand,' said Adam. He looked at the woman talking to him. She was tall, thin, conventionally attractive and talking crap.

'Oxford or Cambridge?'

'Cambridge.'

'Really? You may know a good friend of mine . . . '

Still stuck in nobs' corner and a man dressed in uniform Ralph Lauren Polo was talking to me. Talking to me wearing shades. I watch my reflection in them. He has a moustache and is talking to me about himself. For the past half-hour he had been talking about himself and was content with my odd monosyllabic utterance.

'I'm like that, if I see something I want, I get it, everything has a price, everything, everyone.'

He proceeded to ask me out. 'What are you doing tomorrow evening?'

'I'm busy.'

'And a ticket to see the English National Opera followed by a meal at the best restaurant in this goddamn city isn't tempting.'

'Look Mister I'm not interested.'

'So Babe, name your price.'

'There is none.'

'Fancy a shag?'

'No.'

'From the moment I saw you I said to myself Ian, Ian, this chick is cute.'

From the moment he opened his mouth I thought, Norbert, Norbert but I was nicely spliffed and it has been entertaining watching a crud humiliate himself in front of me. Eventually it sinks in that I'm not impressed so he reacts true to his sex spirit and tells me he was winding me up. He says he's engaged to an Asian beauty, ten times more beautiful than myself with bigger tits, which is saying something. Says I'm making a big mistake and accuses me of leading him on.

I told him any assumptions he had were strictly of his own fantastical making.

I think I should leave.

I am attracted to the far corner, playing ball with sidelong glances but some things just aren't possible. I think he is someone I would like to unravel, maybe I should stay, inch my way over but I really shouldn't, all in good time, good time . . .

A bird's-eye view on a summer night, a rooftop terrace in a trendy London borough. Bea's brilliant party plans worked a treat, even Ludendorff would have been impressed. Sounds proliferate, the clinking of glasses, distant chatter, laughter. Party tapes prepared by Brian were dance inducing and far too much alcohol passed through the vessels of tip-top people who moved erratically to the 70s tune 'Get down on it . . . nah, nah, nah, get down on it . . .' Magnify the bird and the view becomes clearer, a swift conversation caught between a man and a woman.

'Good to see you again.'

'You're leaving?'

'Yeah the bewitching midnight hour.' His finger upon my cheek, brushing against my skin. 'Ash,' he said and then wondered if I thought we would bump into one another again.

'A certainty,' I replied.

And he's playing with me.

'Written in the stars hey.'

'More like a sworn affidavit.'

I think I've said too much.

He looked at me, kissed me lightly on the lips, so soft my skin tingled. Flutterby lips. I left.

Court suit

Marcus was agitated. His look concentrated in contrast with his outward attire, a beige-coloured linen suit with a black T-shirt beneath to keep him cool from the city heat. Paddington Station, dirt dusty, busy bustling, noise polluted and Marcus spotted Gilly before she saw him, she stepped out of the first carriage and he watched her smooth down her ruffled skirt and straighten out the back of her jacket. He raised his hand midway in the air, she noticed almost immediately and directed her feet towards him.

Gilly assured Marcus it was unnecessary, there was absolutely no need for him to go out of his way. She was more than capable of looking after herself, she would grab a cab down to her hotel and then meet him at the mews. Marcus wouldn't hear of it, it was no trouble, besides they could go straight on to court. If they were to have a chance of securing a seat in the public gallery they would have to arrive there early, a large media presence was expected never mind the naturally inquisitive variety of citizen with nothing better to do. It was the first day of the trial, *R.* v. *CC Arles* and Gilly just had to be there. It was only right and proper, after all she was part of the family and no doubt Richard would appreciate some moral support. Gilly had come down to London to dock-watch and witness proceedings. She was almost looking forward to the experience, feelings of trepidation mingled with excitement at the voyeuristic thrill of seeing justice done and all that it entailed.

'Hey ho old girl.'

'Less of the old, Marcus.'

Gilly threw her arms around his neck leaving lipstick smudge marks on close-shaven cheek skin above Marcus's trimmed black beard line. An imperfect imprint and she tissue rubbed it off. One never knows for there is always the possibility of misinterpretation. A married man with lipstick stains, a mistaken mark of impropriety and many years ago, too many to remember, long gone and theoretically forgotten, Marcus and Gilly had lain together for a brief moment.

Family friends overstepping the mark. Gilly was a great friend of his wife, best of the lot. Gilly and Jane grew up together, were married in the same year, married similar men, first-borns birthed the year after and two years later they were on to their seconds. Jane proceeded to have a third but Gilly stopped at two.

'Marcus you are a sweetie.' Gilly linked her arm through Marcus's and they made their way towards a waiting car.

'No trouble at all.'

'I feel I have become an old maiden aunt of the Ridleys. Honestly . . . to be chaperoned here and there, Jane left me at the station early this morning and has promised to collect me.'

A generous offer on condition Gilly managed to attain the necessary information. Jane knew there was someone else. There usually was, but this particular one appeared to be sticking, which was not usual. Jane wished to ascertain if Marcus was being made a fool of, if he'd bitten off more than he could chew.

'I just hope he hasn't gone and done anything stupid like fallen in love.'

'Marcus in love, perish the thought Jane, he's just exercising his ego.'

'Passing fancies are one thing but he has had her in the mews for quite a while and I hope she hasn't become too comfortable.'

'Marcus isn't this exciting? I spoke with Richard last night, he's putting on a terribly brave face. Poor darling, I know he's worried, it's been quite a harrowing ordeal for him. Marcus?'

'Hmm?' He wasn't listening, had been distracted by his own thoughts.

They sat in the rear of the car, Marcus's arm stretched out over the back of the seat and Gilly lifted a compact mirror from out of her bag. She checked her appearance, twist-opened a lipstick, applied a shade of deep scarlet and ran her tongue over her teeth before smacking her lips together, then she tip-touched both ends of her mouth and snapped the case closed. Leaning her head against Marcus's forearm, Gilly turned slightly to one side, to face him. 'So Marcus how are you?'

Aha the interrogation about to commence, Marcus expected to open up and relay his heart's desire. He knew exactly what she wanted to hear and needed to tell someone, otherwise he most probably would not have come to the station to collect her. He could so easily have made an excuse but things were getting out of hand. His muse troubled him, was becoming troublesome.

Gilly would goad him, prod him in the side and demand he succumb to her line of questioning. 'Marcus don't act coy, I'm dying to know, I hear she moved in ages ago and more importantly has not moved out.'

He smiled.

'Well . . . ?'

'Gilly, I'm not sure I want to talk about it.' But he did, he did.

'If you're not going to say anything I will surmise the worst, assume love and berate you all day for being a fool. I will niggle you constantly and become a wholehearted pain.'

Marcus laughed.

'I assume she is beautiful and young.'

'Not so young.'

'Under twenty-five?' Marcus raised his hand.

'Under thirty?'

'Twenty-six, if you must know.'

'Marcus you're slipping, I thought you were strictly a saplings man.'

A woman then, he was seeing another woman, far more dangerous than previously assumed.

'How long has it been going on?'

'Quite a while, two years.'

'I see.' And her perfect plucked brows arched upward.

Marcus was staring out of the window. 'She has me, Gilly . . .'

'But . . .'

'I'm not sure I have her.'

The workings of a woman's mind, a complex thing

indeed, it had Gilly thinking, perhaps this one was playing games, leading Marcus on, hoping she might be the one to cast her net far enough and ensnare him . . . 'Has she mentioned marriage?'

'No.'

'Children?'

'Not a bit of it.'

Well that was a relief.

'And money?'

'Not a factor.'

'Does she tell you she loves you?'

'When I ask. Gilly it's ridiculous, I have become annoyingly possessive, which is really not in my nature. She obsesses me, when I travel I ring her every night, if she's not in I want to know where she has been and who she has been with.'

'And she makes no demands?'

'None.'

She had to be after something, they were all after something, even if they didn't know it themselves. Life's payoffs, give and take.

'Marcus if she's making you unhappy then you are just going to have to get rid of her.'

There were times when Marcus felt innocent with her. A man like himself, in his situation feeling, at his age, pure. And times when he felt so angry, when he wanted to shake her hard and break her bubble. Even naked, lying above her, he could sense her slipping from out of his grasp and she made him feel like nothing. She had him tormented, he was doing his utmost to please her, he would do anything for her, did so much for her and yet the more he did, the more he gave the less of her he had. She told him he expected too much of her.

'I know I should let her go . . . I know I should put a stop to it, I tell myself so every day, I wait for her to slip up, I'm sure she does slip up.'

'You mean . . .'

Things, little things not adding up or missing, signs and Marcus was definitely one to recognise them. It vexed him that he should make demands upon her, demands he could not keep himself. After all he was a married man.

'Marcus for God's sake throw her out, she sounds an absolute horror.'

The car rolled to a stop and Marcus helped Gilly out.

'Oh how disappointing. I was expecting something much more in the way of the Old Bailey.' A modern court building, brown brick unadorned cold. Marcus asked the driver to return at 4.30.

'Shall I be meeting her?'

'No, I told her I was seeing you and she said she'd make herself scarce.'

'There was no need for that.'

'It was her decision. She says it's not right and has no interest in my other life.'

'Other life . . . ?'

'My real life.'

'Get rid of her, Marcus.' It was sounding all too complicated for Gilly, far too intense. Unethical. Jane would not be happy. He was obviously losing in the battle to conquer. It's about power and it's about control and Marcus didn't seem to have either. Gilly would have to convince him to cut his losses and move on.

Pushing through the revolving doors, Gilly and Marcus relinked arms and strode towards the courtroom.

Quack

Donald ducked under a ladder, bad luck, he was pushing it, pushing it, the things a man has to do to make a decent living. Wholly indecent but what the heck, pictures in his pocket rubbing against the top of his thigh, burning a hole therein. In the law of averages it was his turn, wait your time sonny boy, yeah, yeah, sure it was. Bits here and there, work placement, no fee, freelancing, hope of . . . he hadn't had two farthings to rub together for such a long time and now all those college years were about to pay off.

Donald was covering one of the hottest cases, lucky break and it was silly season when the journos beef it up. Donald Leary court correspondent and what would his mammy say? 'My son, a court correspondent for a national newspaper!' that's what she'd say. 'Hasn't he done us proud. Sure we never once doubted he wouldn't.'

An actor versus a drama student. Fun, games and a load of frolics. He'd be back and forth, down in court the whole of the week, if it lasted that long. Courtroom Five crammed, judge, jury, stewards, clerks, barristers, witnesses and pen-pushers by the inkpot quick on the draw, the whirring sound of air conditioning, mixing germs with stories.

First day ceremonial court proceedings with lengthy

opening speeches were an untranscribable waste of time for someone like Donald, amounting to a tedious postponement of the nitty-gritty. Bore no resemblance to TV, to real life. Unedited sleep-sending pronouncements, dull formality and it was Donald's job to condense it into something different, something tangible to neatly fit within column inches, to be typeset in cruder vowels and consonants. Not too many letters in each word, not too many words in each sentence, something appealing to our more base instincts.

In a word, jargon. Then after a hard day's work a jar in the Wig and Crown with the lads. What have you got? have you got? anything juicy, better keep shtoom.

Donald's late, he's late, for a very important deadline, no time to dither . . . hello, goodbye, he's late, he's late, he's late. Deadlines had to be met, his editor's desk lay empty, yearning. He was rushing back to the office, an exclusive in the making.

Donald had done his homework well, tripped down memory lane, stumbled on a story, went down to 'Her' drama college and he had a sniff, couldn't believe his luck, proof of, in his trouser pocket and every picture tells a story, sells a story. He was in dire need of some money 'cause one day, one day, he promised himself to jack in this shit and go highbrow.

Has Donald told you of his heart's desire? Bea knew, she was one of the few.

Bea used to tell Donald he was the most talented person she had ever met.

Donald is a closet novelist. A pile of papers stuffed in his closet, eventually when he got the time he would finish it. It's a great story, a Kerouac of the late 90s, no . . . better. The other night he'd been telling someone, who had he been blabbing to? some drunk, some space cadet, at a party the night before, a magazine launch.

Donald was stinking of bitter juice, vodka pussing from his pores. He was sweating it out, on his haste way back to the office. *Pressé*, in a rush to get his name on the front page, slap the photos on his editor's desk, got to work it well, make sure he didn't get fucked over, it's all so easy to be fucked over. Keep the cards in his hands, not a word to anyone. Turned a corner.

Full circle, Donald had been moping around awhile. Crissy severed ties and it's a struggle to make a name for yourself. Donald fallen, the fallen angel, all the way to the gutter. Up you grow and before you know it, the twinkle in your mother's eye is lacklustre and she's beginning to look old. Her fledgling flown and the goal posts shift, shrink, the playing field just doesn't seem so big any more.

Thus at a magazine launch, the charm alarm on full blast and Donald was ingratiating himself, fuck sakes he needed a job, he needed the cash.

'Bet you're dying to know how well I'm doing?'

The more you say, the more they suss just how screwed

you are, so you hint, insinuate, so button it boyo, keep a lid on it. Busy people don't talk about themselves, did you never notice that? Free drink and you say hello to the in-crowd, the shakers, movers, hoping they didn't see you sneak in the back way, an exchange of words and you take a pill from out of your pocket 'cause it boosts your confidence and you swallow it down with a swig from a cute glass you were thinking of nicking.

Yeah, yeah, sure, you nearly opened your mouth a bit too wide, nearly blew the whole story. That's it, Donald's closet novel, a story about a guy, about his own age, about himself. Get real . . . well maybe, but only the best bits. The character's called Dan. Dan wakes up caked in spew, not sure if it's his own or someone else's. Caked in spew and his head is splitting, sore. Christ the guy is sore, Dan is so sore.

Already too long, already they are losing interest, they want a nice soundbite, yum yum, a mouthful, not too much to chew on. The story of . . . OK . . . a story of a scallywag who wagged his tail once too often it fell off. Perfume without the scent.

Dan goes in search of his manhood. A journey of discovery? Of sorts. Yawn, yawn, no but it's good. It's complex, dark, it's very dark, this guy has been around, has been wagging his tail in every nook and cranny. Dan knows the score, he's the diceman scoring a six every throw. It's warped, it's sick, it'll sell, if it gets written.

If he could only find the time to sit down and write it. A tale of a scallywag in search of his tail. Robbed of his reason Dan takes to the streets, searches out every past woman known. You never know she may be keeping it for him in a soft warm place.

Knob off Crissy told Donald to . . . it could make a good
title. A soundbite.

So . . . and how many times does he have to tell you . . .
Donald was at this party, watching his ex Crissy under the
wings of some other bloke, she was looking well. He hadn't
seen that dress before. Donald E'ed up to the eyeballs, good
no great, no brilliant to feel a rush of passing joy, a dancing
jaw and the dry feel of tongue against his pearly whites. He
liked the taste of smoke hitting off the back of his teeth, the
clammy mouth syndrome.

Crissy told him to quit calling, she didn't want to see him
any more.

Did he get the message? Loud and clear.

You meet someone nice, no really nice and then you've
got to fuck it up don't you? Thing was she'd played him at
his own game and won, how does it feel to be the loser? Tail
between his legs, wagging half-heartedly and Donald looked
to the back burner. Bea was sure to have kept the home fires
smouldering, all he'd have to do was stoke it up a bit.

Shit but you can't depend on anyone these days.

Bea wasn't biting, one for the book and Donald remembered how he used to make her cry. Christ it was so easy, too
easy, he hated her for it. Returned from his studies and the
flat would be clean, didn't have to lift a finger, dinner at the
ready. So weak, so weak, all those comfort traps, so he would
get at her, an accumulation of putdowns, he hated the
thought of being depended upon. Rogue behaviour and
around the ragged rock he ran. The rascal ran straight into

Crissy, she appealed to the free spirit in him. She made no demands, wanted nothing more than a good time.

Then she says she didn't want to see him any more, what the hell was that supposed to mean?

Crissy had gone for a new man, she was wearing a new dress, one Donald hadn't seen her in before. Her new man, the editor of a new magazine, a launch party thrown in its honour. Donald's dishonour, he hadn't even received an invitation so he came through the back way. Off his head on a cocktail of drugs. Crissy saw him, he was really pushing his luck, verbal aggression, use of and Crissy told him where to go, in no uncertain terms she made her point crystal clear.

A turning point for Donald and his luck was about to change.

Crissy was with her new man and Donald merely a struggling journalist. Hacking it and another wad of red bills plop on the good morning mat.

Hack, hack away, and another dinner of beans on toast would have finished him off. Donald was running back to the office to face his editor. College beginning to pay off, he went to 'Her' college tracked down a 'class A' photo. Discovered a tasty tidbit of titbit that could grow and grow. A graduation play and she was obviously talented 'cause she landed the lead part. What a scoop, Donald had done his homework well. 'A plus', a shiny star no less, went all the way back to 'Her' childhood and found a spod claiming he knew her from Baby Infants, willing to talk.

Careful editing and insinuations. Things meaning nothing. Donald was hoping to get the front page, a clap on the back, a contract no less. Now you're talking. That would be nice. Not a word to anyone, don't blow it. Hushed whispers, Chinese whispers, what was said? what was meant? and the implications being it didn't matter, in this day and age who gives a fuck?

Donald was a reporter, no a court correspondent and his mother would be proud of him, yeah, yeah, for sure. Whatever fits the bill, whatever he writes, it wouldn't really matter. The bill, the money already expected, the money he would earn, burning a hole in his pocket.

Sweetcake stalling

I was sitting in a café reading an orphaned paper.

RAUNCHY REVELATIONS IN A KISS AND RAPE TELL ALL!

Front page news.

Donald Leary, a court correspondent, what do you know and the country boy has made good. Donald can go home now, head held high.

Top Totty. Tears or Tease?

It may be hot outside but inside Courtroom 5 it was sweltering on this the first day of the sex trial of CC Arles. Scorching discoveries had judge and jury hot and bothered under their collars and it wasn't due to the weather.

The court heard how Arles and the alleged victim first met after an acting class given by him at her drama college. Extracurricular activity soon led to a brief but passionate affair.

Lust at Lunchtime

A spate of afternoon sex sessions followed. Lunch-hour

202

rendezvous in seedy hotels where the couple performed Oscar-winning sex manoeuvres and romped outrageously drinking champagne and sniffing cocaine. Discovering she wasn't his only leading lady, she branded him a **Rampant Double Crossing Rat** and ended the relationship.

Saucy Secrets of Starlet Stunner!

We tracked down former boyfriend, Rob Watts, a school chum sweetheart. Rob met her in the playground and already 'She was a right goer, a complete nymphomaniac. We used to play Mummies and Daddies all the time, the girl was insatiable, couldn't get enough. Once I suggested a **3 in the bed** romp with her best pal Lucinda'.

Arles' barrister Ms Watkins, an attractive brunette, revealed that only two days prior to the supposed attack the alleged victim had rung Arles. She said she had run into him at a party and he mentioned a part in a play she would be perfect for which he was then rehearsing. The part being **A Saucy French Strumpet!!**

She claims Arles asked her to drop by the theatre to discuss the part and he would try to get her an audition. Asked if it was true she had been unemployed since leaving Drama College, was desperate for work and would stop at nothing to find some she answered though she had been in several fringe productions, she had merely been following up a lead.

The case continues.

We want to know what you think?

Is she a mercenary freeloader who uses men to get on in life, or a poor victim of a vicious rape attack? Call our freephone number and tell us now.

Exclusive photos, double spread centre pages.

She's no prude she's completely nude.
See photos of her in the flesh performing in the sex play *Equus*, where she pranced and frolicked about the stage in her altogether plus having simulated sex in front of an audience.

My mouth agape. Donald Leary sunk way past saving, although it had to be noted he does what he does well, one could hardly tell someone with a brain had written that. Ah he's only making a living. I pushed the paper down the crack between the table and wall.

Best left unread, it was making me nervous.

I was waiting for Bea in a genuine French *pâtisserie*, down Soho way. The proprietress, authentic enough was sufficiently haughty to give me that true Parisienne kickback and looked at me with disdain before handing over a steaming hot chocolate.

Merci buckets and it really was steaming outside, a freak summer storm. Respite from asthma heat that had the city choking, tensed up tight and migrained out of it. Then out of the blue a storm fell, a thrill of rolling thunder in a gathering mist of sky anger. Lottery lighting and it could be you, a lucky strike and the streets emptied pronto. I was wringing, the black clouds broke within eyesight of the café, caught me in sheets of warm city water, rain staining me with collected pollution, my sodden clothes clung tight and I was sporting the wet T-shirt look, perhaps the impetus for Madame's tight-lipped scowls.

What? . . . See . . . see . . . mimicry and I can't help it, sure you only know what you know and these English are getting to me, colonising my thoughts with vulgar vernacular.

A paper left behind on the spare seat beside me, the seat I

was keeping for Bea. I didn't have to read it, had no intentions to, just wished Bea would hurry as the café was over flowing. I live in hope that one day Bea will be punctual. A time is set and I add fifteen minutes, but she sussed me out and has since added a further fifteen. Three times I have vouched for the seat, three times I have pissed people off. If she doesn't come soon I shall get annoyed, I shall forfeit her seat and she can stand in the corner dripping.

Bea shows up. Dry, not one smidgen of damp on her body. On a day that had begun high in the forties Bea just happened to be carrying an umbrella. She pushed the door open and sauntered in. Had waited till the storm was over, had I been there long? Twice as long as usual, oops, sorry. She ordered coffee and cake for two in her 'I am someone to be reckoned with' tone of voice and the French bitch jumped to it. I don't get it, I just don't get it.

'Only a hundred and thirteen shopping days to Christmas,' she informed me.

'Christmas, Christ, Christmas, already?'

Well September actually.

'Brian and I are homeward bound, I'm going to introduce him to the folks. It's all booked and paid for.'

'My thoughts go out to Brian.'

'My mother's not that bad.'

Bea told me her mother was so anxious that Brian be the one, she had enrolled in an 'how not to interfere' part-time evening course.

I said nothing, the cream was sweet and the pastry flaky. My finger dabbed the thin layer of icing dusting the plate as

Bea sucked on a chocolate éclair. The chocolate licked off the outside and the excess cream squeezed until the choux emptied, which she then dunked in her tea.

'I'm such a pig,' admitted Bea.

I said nothing.

She remarked how stressed out I looked and I thanked her profusely.

She said she had something important to tell me and I said snap.

Then she suggested we share another cream cake.

Share? share? Momentarily the old Bea resurfaced and sharing a cream cake with her is two for Bea and one for me. Let's go all out, let's throw caution to the wind and douse ourselves in calories. She smiled slyly then clicked her fingers.

'Waitress.'

'No really,' said Bea, 'you look dreadful,' and she asked me what's up.

Father Bea to the rescue, to comfort a troubled spirit. I winced, she meant well, but to confess would only serve to make her feel better than she already did. But Bea, not one to give up easily, started blagging her way around me, vowing she had in her possession some particularly good news which would cheer me up no end.

I went for the litmus test and asked her to swear on her mother's life which she did with no hesitation. That good, whey hey, but first, but first . . . troubles with Suit not to mention a certain situation.

'I'm moving out, Bea.'

'What?'

I had decided to give my besuited Seigneur his marching orders.

'I'll be destitute, Bea.'

'Makes a change from prostitute.'

Jesus can't a girl get any sympathy. Bea, my one and only friend was slagging me off to my face. She assured me I was doing the right thing and it was about time I picked on someone my own age.

'When are you going to tell him?'

'Tonight.'

Now my turn, my turn, the silver lining after the storm and she commanded me to be patient, be patient.

She pursed her lips and I could tell she was especially gleeful about this slice of upcoming information.

'Guess who called and asked for your number?'

'I give up.'

'No, you can't, you haven't even guessed.'

'Bea I give up, tell me.'

'Adam.'

'And?'

'And nothing till you fill me in on Suit. Every detail, I want to know every painful detail.'

This woman is unbelievable: she had me over a barrel.

Freebasing on the verbal

Day three.

Bound by law, court bound, dressed to convey the truth or what I perceived to be true and though I say it myself I looked rather nice, no matter innocence incarnate, my good self had been called to account for a certain situation. Present by default but present none the less.

'Are you all right, young one?'

'Sure, Mister.'

The security guard and he's asking me if he can be of any help.

'I . . . I'm here for the CC Arles case,' I stammer stutter.

'Oh,' he says and points the way ahead.

I stumble sigh the whole of the British establishment bearing down upon this little mick, what would they make of me, see I've got this massive bomb to drop and I'm just hoping it won't explode in my face.

Swallow your pride, girl.

I go to the noticeboard to read the notices and notice a name I know.

The *R. v. Yobman* and in a blink of an eye, a light's flicker he's there before me with Marla.

'Awight,' she screeches. 'Didn't think I'd see you again.'

'Marla, Christ what's happened?' Her belly protruding outwards and she tells me she's pregnant by Gary.

'Mrs Yobman now,' and her face barely visible through a thick layer of make-up shines proud and she pushes her hand under my nose displaying 24-carat love.

'Congratulations, I hope you'll both be very happy.'

'Eh Gary look who it is.'

He's wearing dark shades and his best suit, probably the one he wore to the wedding. Throws me a nod of acknowledgement and asks me what I'm up for.

'The CC Arles trial, and yourself?'

Theft he declares and everything relating to it. He lists his crimes in legalspeak like he knows what he's talking about.

'Good luck,' I say and Marla pats her stomach:

'We're hoping for community service.'

Sat in the corridor, my thoughts racing, flooding my head and I look at the strange faces passing me by, they have no idea who I am, don't even know my name, well that's my privilege or is it the other way around? Whichever, I'm not so hot on legalities. I sip from a foam cup of coffee, bite into its soft edges, burn my tongue and place the cup on the chair beside me.

I have been questioned and briefed.

I think I know what I am doing here. I think ... of questions posed on quicksilver mercury-tinged tongues seeking answers.

Pre-emptions, pre-emptions and disbelief suspended for what the eye doth see must be true, I think that's some sort of saying, almost positive I've seen it written down somewhere. I hear my name called out, I have been called to present my perspective on the matter, granted permission to speak. See it was a certain situation and way out of my control. Control and it's such a funny thing, is it given or taken or . . .

Whatever, whatever, the heart of the matter is a long way off and what the eye doth see . . .

My name has been called and I am led into the courtroom taking the floor a step at a time, foot raised falling foot raised falling, feeling each movement, the gravitational pull.

Grounded and I am flying.

In dreams I fly, there's no stopping me I heaven soar, hey diddle diddle moon directed and cow jumping over I'm travelling faster than the speed of light, now you see me, now you don't. Can't even keep up with myself, breathless, panting I am breathing again, my lungs creaking and a state of numbness is no good at all.

Centre stage upon a stand, my butterfly stomach churning and I feel like an actor. I spy with my little eye . . .

Bea and she is waving to me in an underhand manner and I'm glad of the support. Of course the lure of meeting CC may have had something to do with it. But she is here in the front row, best seat of the house with Brian beside her and I see her poking her elbow into his side and he winks at me.

I'm on your side girl, and he has said this to me and he has told me how perversely attracted he was to the idea of viewing CC being publicly humiliated, harkening back to events in his youth.

My cocooned butterfly about to break open and I feel sick now, a sharp pain running free. Flashback and under my skin I am zooming over that bridge in grand Munch style.

Marcus is sat two rows back from Bea, looking straight at me, his eyes boring a hole in my head. He leans towards an uptight upright woman and whispers something in her ear. Tut tut there's no need to be rude now is there and I sway from being the headlit rabbit to the oncoming car . . .

. . . To the headlit rabbit, for Donald sits with the hackpack, his notepad in his hand and he is sneering at me, would like to see me come undone. Now's your chance Donnyboy to get me back.

Time's trickery, a sickening reminder of what went before.

It was a long while back, around the time when Donald and Bea were going through their eruptions. That's hardly an excuse for they were always erupting and then one winter night. One winter night we fell into a lustful fit, flung our drunk dampened bodies against one another. There was nothing we could do, the thirst was upon us, we had had to be drunk, would never have done it sober. Inebriety a digestible excuse and in the morning those hangover consequences were watered down.

He rang a couple of times, my accented monosyllabic answers, negative, negative, couldn't believe I'd sunk so low as Bea wept raw on my shoulder.

My shame and then I had to go and better it didn't I? The rot had begun to set in.

Racked with guilt, almost raskolnikovian, a bad, bad, error on my part.

I want the earth to open up and swallow me whole, keep your head, girl, keep your head.

A head . . .

A shape . . . stepping into my line of vision. Thought provoker, head invader and I keep popping up in the most unusual places, in his life and he in mine.

And he in mine, intuition and it comes as no surprise.

I confess wanting so much to know him, Adam and I remember that night clearly. Oh for a right time right place scenario, if only the fates would conspire and in harmony you're dumb struck breast sore. Ah that's the best game of all, 'cause you know you're going to win and then the pump takes control, heart-strings pulling any which way. Yeah my perspective momentarily shifts to the other side to where he is standing, opposite me, opposing me. And for all my flaws I still have this capacity to believe in happy ever afters.

Fuck it.

The good book is placed in the palm of my hand. I read the good book once, guy who wrote it had a great sense of humour, overflowing with role models and Mary Mary quite contrary I guess I opted for the wrong one.

Do you ever get the feeling you're being watched?

Achem a cough to clear my throat
A need to establish some facts
But where to begin?
See the end is in sight it's beginnings that are hard to define, the end is specific, the culmination of an event, but where to begin at what point exactly was the beginning, moreover the beginning of what, but to put a story in a nutshell would ruin it completely, or at the least take away from what is about to happen, although the verb to happen denotes a future and at present all we can deduce is from the past.
See already I'm prevaricating.
Focus girl focus.
OK OK . . . time was when I was impressionable, a man in a suit stopped me in my tracks and he promised me the world. The world on a plate, was he joakanin-ing?
See I had a dream once, Martin Luthered on a star-spangled future and time was ebbing, ebbing away and my innocence fast fading was beginning to stale, my breasts understood the concept of gravity and already lines were forming at the edges of my eyes.
But you know all this.
It was way past midnight and I had just got in, I had fixed myself a drink . . .
. . . yeah in my gush rush to make reality more palatable. Headfirst furiouser and furiouser but from where I was crouching there were no convenient keyholes to peep

213

through. No magic ointment to ease those tired limbs after scrambling over that deep dark continent . . . I I was giddy I . . . I was dizzy, hey and I'm not the only one at it. You've only got to open your eyes. Look around take a peek, escapades of flight on a global scale, truth fleeing to seek comfort in narcotic dream worlds that allow you feel. Alive, special. I was totally out of it, so out of it I lost myself a moment. I was pushing, pushing, Christ I was trying but the odorous stench of doom had latched on to me. I breathed it and it kept me ticking.

There was only one course of action left. I was going to have to start again.

Start again.

Following graduation I spent a year in transit went to the end of the world in search of experience and found it in the form of a most untrustworthy four-letter word. Damn that word, four innocent letters amalgamated into something so hard to define, vowing constancy, then backtracking to bleed you dry. The upshot being I had had enough experience to last me a lifetime and from way down under I was travelling north-westward, tunnelling back with a heavy load. There was a fissure on the outer left side of my heart, it was slowly tearing in . . .

Brian Martin was sitting in Courtroom Five mentally urging the case to get a move on, he wanted the defendant to be sentenced before the day was out as he had arranged a very important meeting the next day. He'd been talking to Bea about his scheme, his plans for the future. The proposed birth of a company, a Berian adventure. He would prove himself a veritable master of design, a match for Bea and another point of commonality could be added to her list. A preliminary five-year plan had been sketched with revolutionary zeal and tomorrow he was going to test the water, an initial meeting organised with his bank manager. A partnership in the process and Bea was going to help him, thought it a great idea. 'Business is in my blood,' she had declared. 'Sure aren't my family in the betting business. I can smell a winner a mile away.'

Brian shifted in his seat, took a tissue from his pocket, carefully blew into it and then checked the time.

. . . Where was I? Ah yes crossing time zones, didn't know where I was exactly, but I was travelling back, a return journey. We met on a plane, it's amazing what you can pick up in foreign climes. Marcus had gone for a stroll down the economy aisles to see what was on offer. Discovered me at the rear complaining to the stewardess about having to sit next to high-time hicks. My outrage clashing with my small frame, torn denims, tatty T-shirt and trussed sneakers. Marcus suggested the empty seat beside him in the executive section, much more comfortable. An irresistible offer and I found myself talking to a most interesting man and found it very flattering that someone of his age and experience took me completely seriously. I told him of my plans, I was planning on staying in England over the summer months, do a bit of temping, save some money 'cause I had this vague idea I wanted to travel round South America. Christ I had so many plans and we talked till touchdown.

My first taste of the rear seat, boy what a difference to backpacking.

We exchanged numbers and then Marcus dropped me to an address I'd been given by a friend already over . . .

Adam had called Bea to ascertain a certain set of numerical digits. On the premise of good manners he had thanked Bea for a lovely evening, scrawled the given number on the back of a dry-cleaning ticket. The night before, held in his hand and Adam hadn't done this sort of thing for so long, felt out of practice, was flicking through the TV channels, nothing of interest to stall him, his whiskey glass empty and his leg bouncing up and down, impatient. He lowered the volume of the television set but before his fingers had lifted the receiver . . . intercepted. She had got to him first.

'Adam.' And he recognised the voice. Straight off, straight down the line.

'Adam, it's Hayley.'

He hadn't expected that.

Fuck it.

He hadn't expected that at all.

She said she was over, was in London for the next couple of weeks, maybe they could meet up, it had been a long time.

'Yeah,' said Adam, 'it's been a while.'

'I just thought it would be a shame to come all this way and not get in touch.'

. . . Marcus told me I was more than welcome to get in touch.

My first taste of London and it didn't go down so well. See that fissure in my heart had become a mighty crack it was ripping me up something rotten.

Guess I was in need of an antidote or at least I was open to it.

Anyhow I put my nose to the grindstone, down on the grindstone and it ground me down. I was living in a shitheap, a highly imaginative selection of different patterned wallpapers torn and peeling with stained carpets, completely lacking in charm, just enough room to touch each wall with outstretched arms and mentally disintegrate.

Next thing I knew I was out of pocket, owed the bank a fortune.

And a lot of water has passed under the bridge.

So I took Marcus at his word and got in touch with him.

In a small bookshop off Charing Cross Road I let Marcus catch my eye.

'Tell me again how old you are?'

'Twenty-four.'

'Twenty-four . . . so very twenty-four, ahh . . .' he threw his head back and sighed.

'Has anyone ever told you how . . . fresh you look, you carry a summer breeze, a cooling tease and it breathes upon my face. You make me smile, you . . .'

I lowered my eyes.

'I'm not that young you know.'

I guess my intense look had him rattled and he bent toward the challenge.

'May I?'

He actually believed I could be his and he was right. He

sized me up and demanded a genetic explanation. I told him
I was expensive.

Hey flattery will take you all the way to nowhere.

Bea had told her mother she was going to court.

'That one was always trouble, you could smell it off of
her.'

'Mother . . .' groaned Bea.

All the same Bea was feeling fairly smug with herself, had
always suspected she had the makings of a detective in her.
Bea had put two and two together. The man in the suit just
sitting behind her was Marcus, it had to be. The woman
beside him kept referring to him by that specific name,
hushed whispers when her friend took the stand. Bea had
never met him before, heard all about him though, but
hadn't expected him to be, well, so handsome, Marcus was
incredibly handsome, especially considering his age.

Dark horse, thought Bea, that one is such a dark horse.

. . . Yeah I can handle it. I can handle it, with the bit
between my teeth and the reins held tight. So there I was,
the first blush of youth still seared across my cheeks, marking
me out.

Objection My Lord and suchlike sayings, men in wigs,
horsehair, starched winged collars, bands and gowns and
everything so proper and in its place. These were the things
Bea expected to behold, ripples of shock, gasps at the scandals

unveiled but the case was proving all a bit mundane. Bea turned her head eighty degrees to get another eyeful of Marcus.

. . . Bea was always on at me about Marcus, informing me I lacked morals.

'Picture the poor little wifey stuck by the hearth with numerous kiddies.'

I informed her his children were older than me.

'No matter. Blindly in love and suffering, suffering because an evil malicious woman has taken Daddy away.'

Yeah like he succumbed to the snare of the originator of sin. Couldn't help it, bless him, he's only a mere mortal.

There is never any point in arguing with Bea, within seconds we regress to kindergarten babes and that time when she accused me of copying her painting as I had drawn a house, a sun and a tree too.

Besides, as Bea says it herself, she *is* usually right and I confess it had crossed my mind and I guess I had copied her painting, an admission yanked from out of me when Bea applied the Chinese burn torture technique to both my arms during elevenses.

Deploring my taste in the other gender, Bea would lecture me regularly in semi-patronising tones.

'What will I do with you? Eh? Eh?'

I mean Bea can't exactly talk, having had a fair share of foul in her time.

More to the point, though you'd never warrant it, was it not only herself who had indoctrinated me in the art of flirting.

The school hall converted into a happening place, paper decorations on the walls and a bunch of braced kids spinning on the floor like glitterballs.

The DJ had set up camp in the corner, a sixth-year student with a semi-decent record collection, chairs shoved to the side, trendy teachers on the prowl and white plastic cups of lemonade. We were mere babes, first-year students, first disco, there's a first for everything. I was pushed up against the wall, flowering. The slow set had been gathering momentum and lucky Bea was in the arms of an older guy, a third-year student with long hair. They moved in rhythm, Bea's head rested on his shoulder while his hands rubbed up and down her in clumsy gropes.

He had pulled Bea tight towards him, later she said she could feel his thingy stiffen and that it was disgusting. Ten minutes of slow dancing, five of which I had already spent hiding out in the toilet. Bea to the rescue and she convinced me to come out, otherwise how would I ever get asked to dance and to smile.

'And don't be picky,' she said reiterating her mother's words of wisdom. 'Better to dance than wilt.' And she gave me a look far beyond her years.

There I was, wishing I had stayed home to watch *Starsky and Hutch*, at the side of the wall sweating, no kitchens at a school Friday night disco. It would end at eleven. Bea's dad had promised to collect us and we told him to park round the corner so we could pick up credibility points on the way.

I wore bright dangly earrings, tight blue corduroy trousers, a dinky belt and white stilettos. I looked hideous and when I looked again Bea had disappeared. She had gone for a necking session out to the gym. The gym was the Love Centre, the place of dreams, the place to be. If you didn't make it to the locker room by the end of the night then you were never gonna make it.

I wasn't going to make it, kinda just slinked around the room as if I was looking for something.

Then . . .

Poked on the shoulder by Pat Flynn, 'Nights in White Satin' blasting away. I was taken aback. Pat was cool, was a smoking, stubby, rugby hard man, all of thirteen years and five foot, always in trouble and already wearing a leather jacket.

'Would you like to dance?' and he wasn't half bad, known as a bully but a little bit of rough never did no one no harm.

'Sure,' I said and my whole self gave a sigh of relief. I'd been saved, saved from the humiliation of being branded a Class A Dog.

Arms placed upon corresponding shoulders but the slow set came to a halt and Metallica was warming up.

'Fuck the dance, let's skip straight to the gym,' I screamed.

Dark and dank and boy smelly, rugby socks and . . . and . . .

I met up with Bea back in the hall, it was five past eleven . . .

'Dad will go apeshit, where the hell have you been?'

I was smiling confidently and confidentially I whispered to her,

'The boys' locker room.'

'Oh my God.' And Bea wasn't impressed. 'You've always got to fuck up don't you?'

'What? what? what have I done wrong now?'

'It's out of bounds unless you're practically married, it's the girls' locker room for snogging.'

'We weren't only snogging,' I boasted.

'I know,' she answered. 'Me along with half the school.'

Yeah I guess I was fairly forward even then.

Anyway my past is hardly relevant.

OK, with respect to Marcus I was hardly what one would call naive.

Then again, and he said it himself.

He said it was about freshness, catching youth before the rot sets in, before life dishes out its inconsiderate amount of pain and chaos. Dissipated youth forming life lines which had been painted in by others were not to his taste. Marcus considered himself a bit of an artist. He liked his canvas clean.

I noted this predilection and noted too that he liked to have purpose in his conquests, was more interested in saving lost souls, steering a girl to her potential.

To be honest I found him very attractive.

Christ he had so much confidence, so much, if only I could leach a little off what difference would it make?

I thought about it, I thought about it a lot.

'Are you appalled?' he asked.

I laughed aloud. Appalled was not the right word and then I ceased laughing, he was serious, wanted to make it a reality. The reality was he paid off my overdraft and ensconced me in a love nest, a gilded cage, my eyes wide open as I walked in willingly.

And in the beginning we did have fun. The rear seat was comfortable, luxurious. It's good to treat yourself once in a while and we dined on tables clothed with linen, bedecked with silver, served by the silent and unseen. We travelled a little, just enough to keep me happy and my wardrobe grew, seasonally changing. Marcus liked to see me dressed well. He liked to look at me, guide me. He told me his life twice over.

Bored I envied his bravado and fortune, the Dick Whittington that he was. Mein own Führer, sweet pappy of mine.

I would sit between his legs, feel his fingers run the length of my spine, my hair, my neck. He would complement my depth of thought, my logic of argument, especially when I reiterated what he had told me, what he had taught me. It gave him pleasure acting the grey-haired guru, he felt needed. He liked me to read aloud to him, his choice of course, something philosophical or high literature. He would listen intently and then question me to see if I had taken it all in. Absorption allowed, encouraged but I could never reveal things he knew nothing of.

'I am too set in my ways to change,' he'd say.

Marcus didn't want to know what I had to offer, only what he could give.

If I didn't know him better, I would say he gave too much.

When we slept together I'd curl up and away. Curled up

over like the red plastic fish from a Christmas cracker, suppressing a rising tide of feeling . . .

Marcus wasn't feeling so well, a slow ache spread across his temples. He had not envisaged such a situation, could not believe she was standing before him and he had known nothing about it. He had spoken of the case to her on so many occasions and yet she had said nothing of her part in it. Nothing. She knew of his dealings on Richard's behalf, of his stance in the matter and then there she was confronting him. Double trouble, his little enigmatic one not so attractive any more, one blow following another and the acid taste of last night's dinner lay in his stomach. She had duped him, dumped him. He cursed his stupidity, had assumed he knew her.

. . . Some time passed before I realised Marcus knew me inside out.

He set me a fine example and I followed his trail, so aptly, so precisely.

Deceit was gnawing at me, altering me into something I wasn't.

Comfortably deviant I was losing myself.

See he took and he left me and he took me and he left me.

A needle on a record stuck, the same loop playing, loop the fucking loop.

It was doing my head in.

And he had me where he wanted me and as he really couldn't bear to share me, I started to fuck around.

Yeah I played by the rules, the best form of sabotage.

And maybe there is an inkling of truth in Ruth's logic. Sexuality is such a fragile thing. So easily crushed.

So often masquerades as power, as . . . as violence does for passion.

His violent passion, her passionate violence . . . Case in point, I mean this is precisely why I find myself here.

For sure and sitting before me is an actor on trial. A trained professional actor whose vocation allows him plenty of pretence, but in reality everything's above board, straight down the line. Those boundaries between reality and escapism are well marked, he marks them well, for sure.

It was merely a misunderstanding of a physical nature.

A passionate lover bares his soul and he says, one must not misunderstand me, those strikes I lashed across her face were affectionate. Affectionate strikes, dry sweeping kisses striking hard . . . and when I clasped a clump of ill-begotten hair and held it my hand . . . it was only a lover's keepsake to entwine in gold or silver and wrap in pretty poetry. Pinches mere marks of testing reality, and when I bit into her, well that was horseplay . . .

Horseplay, physical.

Others prefer to use their heads in such matters,

their tongues . . . wordcracks,
their silence . . . unspoken restraints,
their eyes . . . spying,

Horseplay, a pleasurable game, a timeless pursuit, skin diving, we were jumping off different corners of the board, bending the rules. The rules are bent, the rules are in such disarray . . .

A texture of betrayal clothed Marcus's thoughts. She had so recklessly squandered his trust, his love of her. After all he had given her, all he had done for her, to be spat back in his face. The previous evening she had made him dinner, sat him down to talk to him, she said there was something she needed to get off her chest.

. . . I was eating out of one hand, defecating on the other and neither of us felt like dessert. The words slid off my tongue the last glass of claret burning red, robbing the colour from Marcus's cheeks. I do not doubt that he loved me but badly, so badly and yet he told me, he gave me his word of honour,

'How could I hurt you? I've never hurt anyone in my life.'

'Attempt to think from another perspective, Marcus.'

But he couldn't make the jump.

'Marcus you are a giver of nothing and a taker of the best of me.'

He mustered a retort:

'You are a free spirit, wander where you will.'

'And I will.'

No not all gifts are appreciated, see sometimes, sometimes it's nice to do things on your own. His blank face, his bank balance buoyant and it was time to take account of the situation, to take off those spectacles, those rose-coloured glasses that kept me warped.

It doesn't have to be like this.

My juried past, my private world exploited.

Of course I admit I was co-conspirator, guilty as hell, had sentenced myself to a vacuum. And now?

September and the trees are about to shed their leaves, a new leaf. A beginning to an unspecific end. A definite event happened, a finality has occurred . . . and you stagger on, slow motion snakeskin changing and you stagger forward.

Christ I've been such a sucker.

Courtroom Five

The public prosecutor approaches the stand and I dread the thought of hearing my own voice and he asks me to tell the court about a certain situation.

. . . I've told you, I'm sure I've told you before it was way past midnight and I'd just got in. I ran myself a bath and fixed myself a drink.

Strange and I heard a muffled holler and went to take a peek, thought it was myself coming from within, get out of this situation girl you're in the wrong place, wrong scenario . . .

Eye, eye?

I spy with my little eye . . .

She was looking real fine, short skirt, high heels, no matter and he was walking close behind, so close, he grabbed her hand, swung her round, he was all over her, she disappeared inside his coat and he enveloped her.

I thought they were enacting some sort of scenario.

These days there's no telling what's what.

Think straight . . . linear thoughts but there's an infinite number of points upon a line, I mean you can so easily veer off course get a little twisted although you've got to draw the line somewhere or at least get to the point. The point being self-evident. Self-evidence, evidence of being so I could feel a little control, power.

I stood by the window jealous, I wanted that passion, I wanted that hunger to be quenched.

Hey a little bit of rough and tumble never did no one no harm.

No, no and I'd got it all wrong, all out of proportion.

And so numb, must have seen too many late night TV shows.

The youth of today hey and I went back to my running faucets, bubble bath, the clock ticking morning forward. The water drowning siren screams, perhaps I don't know, except I went downstairs again. That's it, I had forgotten to bring a towel with me.

Swish of a curtain to blur my vision.

Sat on a kerb smoking a cigarette watching her fade from reality.

He was smoking a cigarette playing with one of her shoes and I thought that odd, she had left one of her shoes behind.

Light in window, looked up.

Oh . . .

Did he catch my eye or did I catch his?

No matter.

And he smiled over to me. He looked at me. He looked at me. No matter.

Swish of a curtain to ease my conscience.

Something had definitely happened.

Then the next morning head down work headed I glanced a fallen programme, a show on a road, and I was certain I'd seen his face before.

Night before.

I shrugged it aside, I shrugged myself aside.

Yet I kept coming back to the same point in time, tripping up on that night in question, it started to eat away at me, just things pointing to it.

I knew what I'd seen I shouldn't have witnessed.

Or rather I had witnessed something I shouldn't have seen.